100 Classic Napkin Folds

100 Classic Napkin Folds

simple and stylish designs for every occasion

Over 700 step-by-step photographs show you how
to make stunning folds to a professional level

Rick Beech

southwater

This edition is published by Southwater, an imprint of
Anness Publishing Ltd, Hermes House, 88–89 Blackfriars Road,
London SE1 8HA; tel. 020 7401 2077; fax 020 7633 9499

www.southwaterbooks.com; www.annesspublishing.com

If you like the images in this book and would like to
investigate using them for publishing, promotions or
advertising, please visit our website www.practicalpictures.com
for more information.

UK distributor: Book Trade Services; tel. 0116 2759086;
fax 0116 2759090; uksales@booktradeservices.com;
exportsales@booktradeservices.com
North American distributor: National Book Network;
tel. 301 459 3366; fax 301 429 5746; www.nbnbooks.com
Australian distributor: Pan Macmillan Australia;
tel. 1300 135 113; fax 1300 135 103;
customer.service@macmillan.com.au
New Zealand distributor: David Bateman Ltd;
tel. (09) 415 7664; fax (09) 415 8892

Publisher: Joanna Lorenz
Editorial Director: Helen Sudell
Editors: Simona Hill and Elizabeth Woodland
Designer: Lisa Tai
Cover Designer: Nigel Partridge
Production Controller: Claire Rae
Photography and Styling: All photography by Mark Wood
and styling by Helen Trent except for the following: Spike
Powell and Andrea Spencer 8, 9, 24, 26t, 27b, 33t, 37t, 38l,
39tr, 40, 51tr, 61, 67, 77, 117tl, 117tr, 119, 123t, 125t, 145tr,
145tl, 149t, 152t, 155.

ETHICAL TRADING POLICY
Because of our ongoing ecological investment programme,
you, as our customer, can have the pleasure and reassurance of
knowing that a tree is being cultivated on your behalf to
naturally replace the materials used to make the book you are
holding. For further information about this scheme, go to
www.annesspublishing.com/trees

Previously published as part of a larger volume, *The Complete
Illustrated Book of Napkins and Napkin Folding*

PUBLISHER'S NOTE
Although the advice and information in this book are believed
to be accurate and true at the time of going to press, neither
the authors nor the publisher can accept any legal responsibility
or liability for any errors or omissions that may have been made
nor for any inaccuracies nor for any loss, harm or injury that
comes about from following instructions or advice in this book.

Contents

Introduction 6
Inspirational ideas 8

EASY FOLDS FOR ANY TIME 10
Diagonal roll 12
Folded roll 13
Candy cane 14
Double scroll 15
Night light 16
Scroll 17
Gathered pleats 18
Paper heart 19
Ice cream cone 20
Geometric style 21
Fanned pleats 22
The flag 23
Envelope fold 24
Breeze 25
Starfish 26
The wave 27
Knotted napkin 28
Wings 29
Sailing boat 30
Pure and simple 31
Cockscomb 32
Pure elegance 34
Duck step 35
Lover's knot 36
Clown's hat 38
Diamond 39

FANS AND PLEATS 40

Mathematics for concertina pleats 42
Napkin ring 43
Bishop's hat 44
Festival 45
Iris in a glass 46
Spiral ribbon 47
Palm leaf 48
Morning sun 49
Double fan 50
Fanned bow 52
Spreading fan 53
Springtime 54
Parasol 56
Knotted ribbon 57
The fan 58
Fire 60
Double jabot 62
Diamond breeze 64
Scallop 65
Chevrons 66
Cream horn 68
Spear 69
Flowerbud 70
Tulip 72
Cicada 74
French lily 76

NAPKINS FOR SPECIAL EVENTS 78

Heart 80
The knot 81
Valentine rose 82
Easter bunny 84
Coronet 86
The swan 88
The corsage 90
Candle fan 92
Butterfly 94
The duck 96
Turbo 98
The dog 99
GI cap 100
Flame 101
Samurai helmet 102
Mr spoon 104
Ocean liner 106
Fish 108
Christmas tree 110
Christmas candle 111
Christmas stocking 112
Christmas star 114

COMPLEX FOLDS 116

The slipper 118
Water lily 120
Mitre 122
Carousel 124
Nautilus shell 126
Overcoat 128
Pinwheel 130
The shirt 132
Bow tie 134
Papillon 136
Oriental fold 138
The place mat 139
Rose 140
Pyramid 142

POCKETS AND PARCELS 144

Buffet parcel 146
Picnic set 147
The cable 148
Envelope 150
Decorative pocket 151
Japanese pleats 152
Cable buffet 153
Gift-wrapped 154
Parcelled surprise 155
Place card holder 156
Bread basket 158

Index 160

Introduction

Crisp, freshly laundered napkins are an essential feature of every well-set table. They may be pressed in large plain squares and laid at each place with the minimum of fuss and for the maximum effect. Alternatively, they may be folded in a variety of ways to complement the food, table layout and occasion. Try some of the innovative ideas in the following chapters and use them as a source of inspiration for developing your own individual napkin art.

Perfect napkins

For folding purposes, choose heavy linen as it becomes crisp when starched. Plain dinner napkins are best and essential for many complicated folding techniques. Regardless of the simplicity of the meal, fabric napkins must be spotless and well pressed. If you are using napkins with a prominent pattern, these should be folded very simply, whereas plain linen or paper napkins are better suited for more elaborate and unusual folds.

Party napkins

Paper napkins are more practical than fabric ones for parties as you can dispose of them quickly and easily. Choose paper napkins that are large and fairly thick, as the thin, small paper ones are likely to disintegrate easily.

For informal parties, use a good selection of different coloured paper napkins; pastels or primary colours both work well. Fold them in half, then overlap them in a large basket and fold one napkin into a lily or tulip shape for the centre of the arrangement.

Paper napkins are also practical options for informal barbecues, especially when sticky spare ribs and other finger foods are on the menu. When laying a garden table, allow two or three different coloured napkins for each place setting.

If you are preparing a buffet it is a good idea to have lots of spare paper napkins to hand to deal with any spills. Bear in mind that guests rarely retain their napkins after the main course and many take a second for dessert.

Left Two different coloured napkins makes a perfect combination for a formal dinner occasion. When used together these contrasting colours give a modern and Oriental feel.

Right *A flowerbud is a simple way to add a finishing touch to a table setting. The delicate design of this paper napkin is the perfect accompaniment to a summer's lunch.*

Left *This is a practical and attractive way to keep table cutlery neat and tidy. The pocket could also be used to display place cards at a formal dinner party, or favours at a wedding reception.*

Using this book

Packed into this book you'll find a host of creative ways to use napkins in a wide range of settings and for any occasion, from weddings and dinner parties to barbecues and picnics. There are 100 beautiful and practical projects that show how to create a variety of stunning table displays, and each stage is illustrated and carefully explained so you too can achieve expert results.

The projects are divided into five sections. The first section, *Easy Folds for Any Time*, features simple folds such as the Diagonal Roll, Folded Roll and Sailing Boat. In the second section, *Fans and Pleats*, you will find slightly more advanced ideas such as the Bishop's Hat, Iris in the Glass and The Fan. The third section, *Napkins for*

Below *Red is the perfect colour for a festive table setting. Stunning silver tableware and decorations complement the folded napkin beautifully.*

Special Events, features elegant ideas, perfect for formal dinner parties, such as a Butterfly, Easter Bunny and a Christmas Star. The fourth chapter, *Complex Folds*, includes elaborate and unusual designs such as The Place Mat, a Rose and a Pinwheel, and in the final chapter, *Pockets and Parcels*, you will find a delightful selection of practical and novel ideas such as a Decorative Pocket, Picnic Set and a Bread Basket.

It is advisable to start off with the simpler designs in the first chapter before moving on to more complicated designs, and before you know it, these beautifully presented ideas will transform the way you think about napkins and add a fresh dimension to all your meals.

Inspirational ideas

The elegant symmetry of traditional napkin folds is most apparent when they are executed using plain linen napkins. The quality of good linen is shown to its best advantage and the crisp folds, tucks and pleats are beautifully defined in pure white fabric. Coloured napkins can be used to give a more contemporary look or to fit in with a particular theme or occasion.

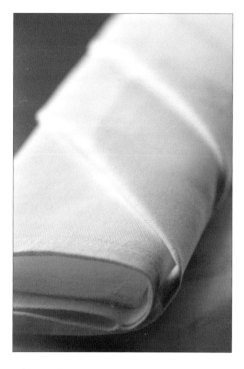

Above *The understated Cable contrasts well with an elaborately decorated table.*

Above *The Cockscomb is a flamboyant and impressive design.*

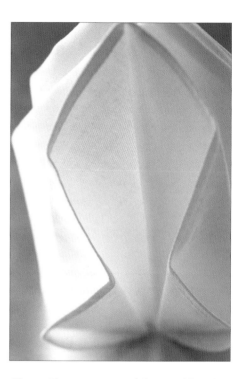

Above *The symmetry of the Double Jabot is ideal for very formal tables.*

Above *Chevrons, a neat and simple design, shows off exquisite hemming.*

Above *The simple profile of the Clown's Hat looks effective in large numbers.*

Above *The French Lily is a classic fold with heraldic roots, perfect for a formal table.*

Above *The Lovers' Knot has a modern look when an elegant napkin is used.*

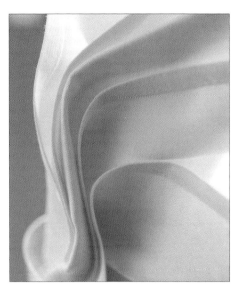

Above *The Flame is a sophisticated design, spectacular in a plain setting.*

Above *The classic Mitre is the stately king of traditional napkin folds.*

Above *The Wave is an understated, smart design that looks contemporary and is easy to achieve with precision.*

Above *The Diamond is a complex and impressive fold, equally suited to traditional or contemporary table settings.*

Above *The Opera House is a modern design with a witty flourish.*

Above *The Fan is a traditional fold that has a charming simplicity.*

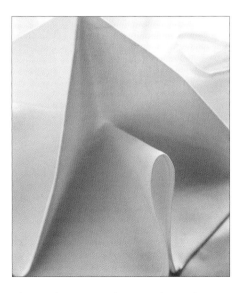

Above *The Carousel is complicated to fold but is a very effective design.*

Easy folds for any time

These neat, elegant folds will bring a little elegance to your table without going over the top. Any one of them would make a thoughtful finishing touch on a table set for a festive family lunch or dinner with friends. It's a good idea to master some of these simple designs before moving on to the more complicated folds later in the book.

Diagonal roll

Rolling fabric is easy, but to keep the roll looking pristine you need to use plenty of starch so that the napkin keeps its crispness. This simple roll is a good choice for a small napkin in fine cotton organdie, which will make a slim shape. A diagonal approach gives an interesting finished outline.

1 With the napkin opened out, right side down and pressed flat, begin rolling it up tightly from one corner. Stop just before you reach the halfway point and hold the roll steady.

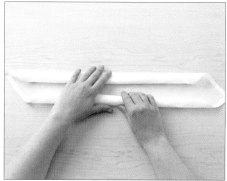

2 Turn the napkin and roll up the other half to match the first side.

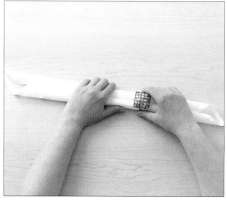

3 Slide a napkin ring over the rolled napkin and position it as desired on the dinner plate.

Folded roll

This is an easy design to master and make consistent for a whole set of napkins, and it works well using either fabric or soft, thick paper napkins. Begin with a well-pressed napkin and match the corners carefully when making the initial fold. Have a napkin ring to hand to hold the roll in place.

1 Fold the napkin in half diagonally to make a triangle, matching the corners.

2 Roll the napkin tightly, beginning at the longest side of the triangle.

3 Carefully fold the roll in half and secure it with a napkin ring.

Candy cane

For this simple but effective design you will need two fabric or paper napkins of the same size but in different colours. Try using one plain and one patterned napkin, or two strongly contrasting shades.

1 Open the two contrasting napkins and arrange them with right sides down, slightly offset and with the top one higher, so that about 2.5cm/1in of the edge of the lower napkin is visible.

2 Starting with the visible corner of the lower napkin and holding the two napkins together, roll them up tightly, keeping the roll horizontal.

3 As you continue to roll the napkins into a long thin cylinder, the colours and patterns of both will create a striped effect on the outside.

4 Carefully bend the roll in half at the centre, pinching a crease to keep the roll set in a V-shape when laid on the plate or table.

Double scroll

This minimal, tailored design would suit a Japanese-style table setting. You could if you wish position the napkin horizontally on the plate and stand a place card between the two rolls.

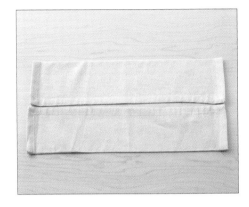

1 Press the napkin flat and, with the right side down, fold in two edges to meet in the centre. Press the folds carefully.

2 Roll the napkin up neatly from one short edge, making sure the folded edges stay flat. Stop rolling when you reach the halfway point.

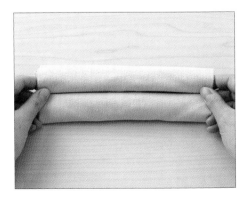

3 Turn the napkin round and roll up the other side. Check that the two rolls match exactly. Hold both rolls at each end to move the napkin to the table.

Night light

Use a fabric napkin for this design – there is too much folding for a paper napkin and it might tear. The napkin doesn't need starching.

1 Open out the napkin and arrange it as a diamond. Fold it in half from bottom to top to create a large triangle. Fold down both layers so that the top corner of the triangle comes to the centre point of the long folded edge.

2 Fold down the top 3cm/1¼in of the short top edge of the napkin. Repeat, folding the napkin evenly until the last fold meets the long edge.

3 Turn up the left-hand end of the folded strip. This end will represent the flame of the night light.

4 Beginning at the turned-up end, roll up the folded strip tightly. When you reach the end, tuck it into the roll at the base of the night light to hide it and secure the roll. Arrange the protruding end so that it resembles a flame.

Scroll

This rolled design makes a small, compact shape, which will sit neatly on a side plate. It is a good way to arrange soft, loosely woven napkins that are not suitable for more sculptural forms.

1 Open out a large napkin and press it flat. Fold the bottom third up, then fold the top third down over the first fold.

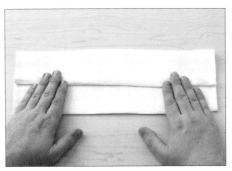

2 Turn up a narrow hem on the top layer. Fold this over twice to make a band across the centre of the napkin.

3 Turn the napkin over so the hem is underneath, and roll it up tightly from one short end.

Gathered pleats

This simple unstructured design using a napkin ring looks pretty as part of an informal table setting.
Use it for napkins that have a decorative border, as it creates a feminine, frilled effect.

1 With the napkin opened out and the right side uppermost, take hold of the centre and lift it towards you.

2 Allow random soft pleats to form as the edges of the napkin fall, and grasp it loosely around the middle.

3 Slide a napkin ring over the gathers to hold them in place and spread out the folds to form an attractive shape.

Paper heart

This understated design is perfect for a paper napkin, though it works equally well with fabric, bringing a light-hearted touch of romance to the table for an anniversary, Valentine's Day, or just for fun.

1 Open out the paper napkin so that it is double, with the long folded edge nearest you. Pick up the bottom right-hand corner and bring it across the napkin, folding from the centre of the lower edge so that the two sides of the folded section are at equal angles. Press in place.

2 Now bring the bottom left-hand corner up and over the first fold, again folding from the centre point. Align the edge of this fold with the edge below it.

Ice cream cone

Use a plain white or coloured linen napkin for this elegant fold so that its clean geometric lines can be clearly seen.

1 Fold the napkin into quarters with the second fold at the lower right-hand side. Fold the two top layers down to meet the bottom corner.

2 Turn the napkin over. Fold the left side two-thirds of the way over the napkin.

3 Fold the right-hand edge in over the previous fold to align with the edge.

4 Tuck the corner of the upper section over the fold beneath it to secure.

Geometric style

Eye-catching and elegantly precise, this contemporary design calls for napkins with a crisp finish in a plain colour or a simple pattern, and is well suited to informal entertaining.

1 Fold the napkin diagonally across the centre, with wrong sides together, to form a triangle.

2 Fold the sloping sides down from the top point so that they lie vertically together along the centre line.

3 Fold the two sloping edges into the centre again from the top point so that they meet at the centre line.

4 Turn the napkin over and fold it in half. Tuck the long point into the horizontal fold and turn back again.

Fanned pleats

This is a quick and easy design for the beginner, ideal for a small napkin with interesting decorative detailing. For a more slender shape, you can fold the left-hand edge in under the three pleats.

1 Arrange the napkin diagonally, right side down, and take the bottom corner to the top to make a triangle.

2 Folding from the centre point of the long edge, take the left-hand point across to the right, offsetting it slightly so that it lies about 2.5cm/1in above the lower point.

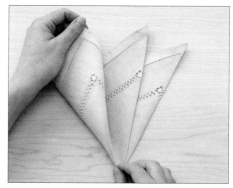

3 Bring the remaining (centre) point of the napkin over in a similar fashion to make the third pleat.

The flag

The triangular shape and multiple points of this asymmetrical design recall a series of fluttering pennants. The underlying straight edge is slightly rolled to represent a flagpole.

1 Fold the napkin in half from top to bottom. Pick up the top layer of the bottom left corner and take it across to the right-hand corner.

2 Turn the napkin over and repeat on the other side to form a triangle. Fold the whole thing in half from right to left.

3 Arrange the four points of the folds so that they are evenly staggered.

4 Roll the vertical edge under the napkin and twist slightly to create the flagpole.

Envelope fold

Eminently elegant, this fold can be accomplished in a trice and is ideal when you are in a hurry but want to make an impression. It looks smartest in pure linen, which falls naturally into soft folds.

1 Fold the napkin in half to form a large rectangle. Next, form a point at one end of the rectangle by folding down each corner toward the centre. This creates the flap of the envelope.

2 Fold the other end of the rectangle over to cover the pointed end. Fold down the corners of this top layer so that it forms a second point lying over the top of the first one.

3 Fold the top point over so that it lies just over the straight folded edge. Crease the fold with your thumb. Bring the second flap over the first and arrange it so that it lies slightly further back than the first, with both points visible.

Breeze

This seemingly artless arrangement gives the impression that a gentle movement of air has caught the layers of the napkin and casually flipped them over, like a breeze riffling the pages of a book.

1 Fold the napkin into quarters, with the second fold at the bottom and the four corners at the top right of the square.

2 Fold the napkin in half again, taking all the layers of the right-hand vertical edge across to the left.

3 ◁ Holding the edges together at the bottom left, take the uppermost corner and peel the top layer over to the right, without flattening the fold.

4 ▷ Repeat with the three remaining layers, making each fold a little shallower to create a layered effect.

Starfish

When you want to add a little height to your table design, but are pushed for time, use the starfish, a chic triangular fold with a well-spread base that allows it to stand up. The starfish is a stylish, unfussy design that looks great when repeated down the length of a long, thin table.

1 Fold the napkin in half diagonally to make a large triangle with the long folded edge at the bottom. Holding the centre point of the lower edge, fold the two sharp points up to the top, so that the edges meet in the centre.

2 Turn the napkin over, keeping it the same way up, and fold the closed point at the bottom to meet the open points at the top.

3 Fold the right-hand half of the triangle over to the left along the centre line.

4 Rotate so that the open edges are at the bottom, and allow the points to spread out to make the standing shape stable.

The wave

Smart yet simple to do, the wave has a tailored look that gives the table an elegant finish. It is an excellent choice when you are entertaining a large party of guests as it is quick to fold and easy to make consistent. Crease the folds very lightly to retain the curves of the wave-like layers.

1 Fold the top third of the napkin down and the bottom third up over it.

2 Fold in a short hem at each end of the rectangle.

3 Fold the left-hand edge across to the right, stopping a little short of the edge to leave a border.

4 Take the new left-hand edge across, leaving a similar border, to create a layered effect.

Knotted napkin

Tying a knot seems one of the easiest ways to arrange a napkin, but making each knot look elegant may take a bit of practice. This style works best with an unstarched napkin made of a soft fabric.

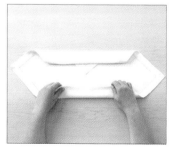

1 If you are using a large napkin, turn in two opposite corners a few times to make the fabric more manageable.

2 Grasp the two turned-in edges and pinch them gently together in the centre.

3 Keeping hold of the centre of the napkin, form a loose knot with the two ends.

4 Pull the ends gently so that the knot has some shape but is not tight.

Wings

This light-hearted design works best with a stiff cotton napkin and is quick to capture the imagination of guests, particularly of young children, as it resembles a butterfly settled on a plate.

1 Fold the upper and lower edges to the centre, then take the lower edge to the top, folding in half lengthwise.

2 Fold the right-hand edge a third of the way to the left.

3 Double this edge back to the right, creating a pleat. Repeat the last two folds on the left side.

4 Push the lower corners of the upper layers inwards. The thickness of the fabric should lift the "wings" slightly.

Sailing boat

This jolly arrangement is perfect for a waterside meal, but even if you are not within sight of the sea you can bring out the marine theme by decorating the table with related pieces such as shells and pebbles.

1 Fold the napkin into quarters with the open corners nearest you. Fold them up to the top point.

2 Fold the sloping sides downward from the top point so that the outer edges meet in the centre.

3 Turn the napkin over, keeping it the same way up, and fold up the lower section. Fold the triangular shape now formed vertically along the centre.

4 Hold with the open edges uppermost. Carefully tease out one of the loose points from the tapered end of the boat, to form the "sail".

Pure and simple

As its name suggests, this design is quickly arranged and pleasing to the eye. The result focuses attention on one corner, so it is particularly effective for napkins with a lace trim or embroidered motif.

1 Open out the napkin and arrange it diagonally, with right side down. If there is a motif in one corner place this at the top. Take the bottom corner to the top and press the fold to make a large triangle. Holding the centre of the bottom fold, take the sharp left-hand point up to meet the top corner of the napkin.

2 Repeat with the other side so that the edges meet in the centre.

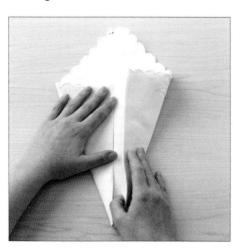

3 ◁ Take the left side of the diamond and fold it in from the bottom so that the edge aligns with the centre. Repeat on the other side to make a kite shape.

4 ▷ Turn the napkin over. Turn up the bottom point and press in place.

Cockscomb

This is an impressive fold that is very effective for small, intimate occasions. A few of these flamboyant cockscombs on the table transform the simplest setting into something special.

1 Fold the napkin into quarters, and arrange it so that the open corners are at the bottom, nearest you.

2 Take the four open corners up to the top, folding the napkin into a triangle.

3 Holding the top corner, fold the right-hand sloping edge downward to lie along the vertical centre line.

4 Repeat on the other side to make a kite shape, making sure the sides and corners meet accurately.

5 Fold the two triangular tabs at the bottom up at the back of the large triangle.

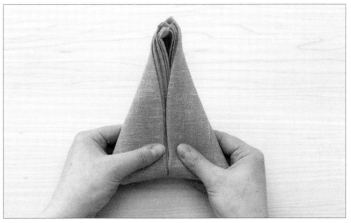

6 Keeping hold of the tabs at the back, bend the sides of the triangle back, folding vertically along the centre line.

7 Arrange the napkin horizontally with all the individual layers lying along the upper edge.

8 Holding the lower edge firmly in one hand, use the other to tease out the layers one at a time, arranging them with a similar space between each.

Pure elegance

This dignified design is equally suitable for formal occasions and low-key meals. Its triangular shape and broad base makes it very stable and it is easy to construct.

1 Open out the napkin with right side down. Fold the bottom edge up by a third and fold the top third down over it. Fold in the short sides of the resulting rectangle to meet in the centre.

2 Fold the upper corners diagonally down to the centre line.

3 Turn the napkin over from side to side, keeping the point at the top.

4 Turn in each end of the long side and tuck one end into the pocket in the other; this forms the back of the design. Turn the napkin over and stand it up.

Duck step

Though it is really a very abstract shape, the duck step is appropriately named. It is a basic napkin fold that is geometrically pleasing and easy to construct but gives a satisfyingly three-dimensional result.

1 Fold the napkin in half bottom to top, then fold the lower edge to the top once more.

2 Holding the centre top point, fold the right-hand upper edge down to lie along the centre line.

3 Repeat with the remaining side so that the edges meet. Turn the napkin over, keeping the point at the top.

4 Lift the top section so that it stands upright. Fold it back slightly so that the "feet" splay and it stays standing.

Lover's knot

A neat twist on every plate looks elegant and modern in a contemporary setting. This very orderly knot is a tidy way to arrange large napkins, and looks especially good when executed using brightly coloured plain napkins, which allow its symmetry and sharp contours to speak for themselves.

1 Open the napkin with right side down and fold it in half, taking the bottom up to the top edge. Press the crease.

2 Double the napkin over lengthwise once more to establish the central crease. Open out this second fold again.

3 Turn up the bottom folded edge to align with the creased centre line.

4 Fold down the open edges at the top to meet the folded edge in the centre.

5 Fold in half again lengthwise, folding from top to bottom to give a neat finish on the outer edges of the knot.

6 Fold down the right-hand half so that the folded edge is vertical, half the width of the strip away from the centre.

7 Fold the left half of the strip down from the same point on the top edge, folding it back (this end will appear longer).

8 Fold the longer end of the strip back a second time, swinging it to the front to lie on top of the right-hand section.

Clown's hat

Tall clowns' hats look wonderful standing on plates along the length of a dinner table. Their unfussy silhouette works well when multiplied. Alternate napkins in two different tones to create a light and shade effect with these distinctive shapes.

1 Fold the napkin in half top to bottom, then fold the top right-hand corner down so that the edges align at the bottom of the napkin.

2 Fold the right-hand triangle over to the left along the centre line, again aligning the lower edges.

3 Bring the upper left-hand corner over to the lower right. Holding the side, place your hand inside to open the "cone".

4 Carefully turn the lower edges out to create a "brim" around the hat. This also locks the folds together and creates a stable shape that will stand up.

Diamond

The diamond is not ostentatious but is seriously chic and will add flair to the smartest of tables. Using very few folds it cleverly creates a small square set diagonally on top of a larger one.

1 Fold down the top third of the napkin, then fold the bottom third over it. Fold in the two left-hand corners to meet each other, as if making a paper plane.

2 Fold the right-hand portion of the strip down at 45 degrees, aligning the upper edge with the edges of the two small triangular flaps.

3 ◁ Fold the top section over at 45 degrees to the right-hand corner. This will create the small diamond for the top.

4 ▷ Fold the remainder of the napkin underneath, so that the crease runs under the lowest corner of the diamond.

Fans and pleats

Once you have mastered some of the classic simple shapes you may want to try your hand at more ornate pleated and layered designs. Any one of these would create a stir at your table. Precise folding is vital to achieving a perfect finish, so some simple calculations may be needed before you begin, to guarantee beautifully even pleats.

Mathematics for concertina pleats

For many of the pleated designs in this book you may simply "concertina-pleat" the napkin randomly from bottom to top in a familiar "fan" style, folding the lower edge over to create a horizontal border, then doubling the material back and forth upon itself. However, for a more accurately folded design, you may prefer to use the following mathematical method, which is much-used in origami. The principles are illustrated here using a square of paper, but the same method can be applied to napkins, whether paper or fabric, and whether the pleats are arranged diagonally or horizontally. The process involves folding and unfolding several horizontal creases, depending on how many divisions you need to make.

1 Fold and unfold the square diagonally in half both ways to find the centre.

2 Fold the lower corner to the centre, then unfold.

3 Repeat with the upper corner. The resulting creases divide the square horizontally into four equal sections.

4 Fold and unfold the upper and lower corners to the first horizontal crease.

5 Take the lower corner and fold it across the centre line to the quarter line at the upper end of the diamond. Repeat with the upper corner.

6 The unfolded diamond will be creased horizontally into eighths.

7 ◁ Turn the paper over keeping the eighths creases horizontal. Fold and unfold upper and lower corners to the eighths.

8 ▷ Continue this process logically until you have divided the square into sixteenths.

Napkin ring

You can apply the method of folding equal divisions shown opposite to create a wonderful napkin ring. Use it to hold an elegant rolled napkin or to secure one of the designs in this book.

1 Divide the square of paper diagonally into sixteenths and make the concertina folds from one corner into the centre.

2 Repeat the folds on the remaining half of the paper. Note that the central diagonal remains unfolded, so the final strip is two sixteenths wide.

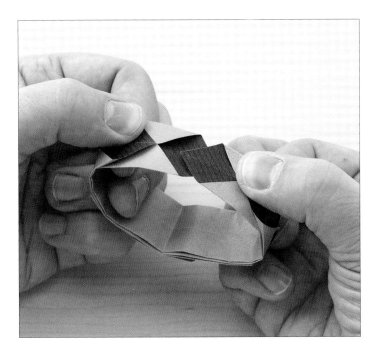

3 Carefully flatten all the creases, then turn the strip over and roll it around your hand into a ring, tucking one end into the folds created by the pleating at the other end. The outside should appear as a succession of alternate diamonds and triangles.

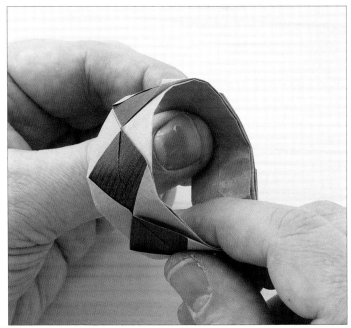

4 Carefully shape the ring. The tension and curve of the paper will ensure that the design stays together.

Bishop's hat

This is a traditional method of folding large dinner napkins, and stands very securely. The proportions are important, so it may be necessary to adjust the spacing of some of the folds to suit your particular napkins as you work through the steps.

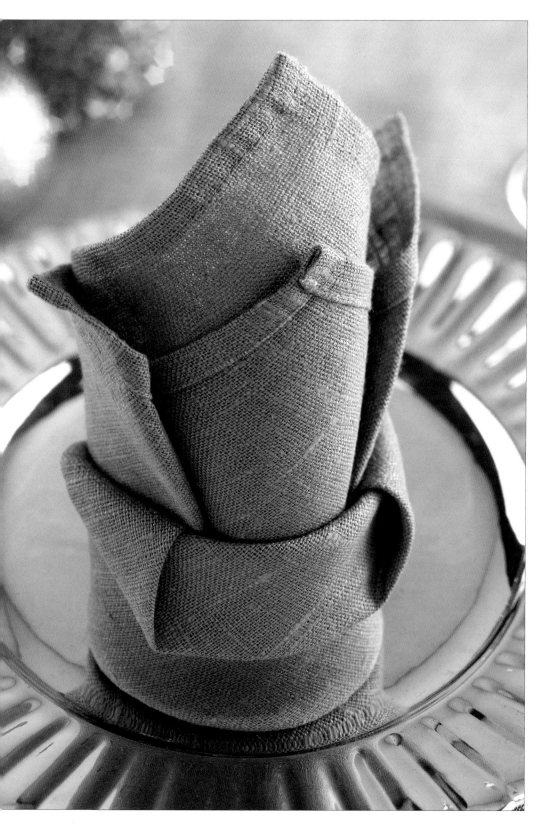

1 Arrange the napkin diagonally and fold it almost in half, taking the bottom corner not quite to the top but leaving a slender border around the upper edge.

2 Fold the lower corners toward the top, leaving a small space between them.

3 Fold the bottom corner up, again taking it not quite to the top corner.

4 Fold the same corner back down, leaving a border at the bottom of the napkin. Turn the napkin over and roll into a cylinder, tucking the corner at one end into the pocket at the other.

Festival

The billowing, flame-like pleats of this bold fan design make it an ideal choice for colourful napkins and lively occasions. Use firmly woven fabric that will hold the pleats, but keep the creases soft.

1 Arrange the open napkin as a diamond and fold the top corner down to meet the point nearest you. Fold down a pleat along the long edge.

2 Make concertina pleats all the way to the corner, keeping the pleats even. Flatten them with your hand but do not press them.

3 Fold the pleated napkin in half so that the two ends of the long edge meet. Pinch at the base to hold the shape and arrange on the table, allowing the pleats to fan out a little.

Iris in a glass

This design creates a very striking display if folded using large, colourful napkins. Arranged in a row of elegant stemmed wine glasses, the folded napkins resemble stately garden flowers.

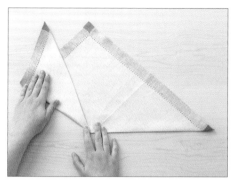

1 Arrange the open napkin in a diamond shape right side down and fold the bottom corner up to the top, matching the hems. Holding the centre point of the long lower edge, fold the two sharp points upward at an angle, leaving an equal space between each point and the central corner. Press the folds.

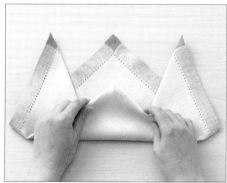

2 Fold the lower corner to the halfway point and turn the napkin 90 degrees.

3 Concertina-pleat vertically across the folded napkin, making about six pleats. Place the pleated napkin in the glass and shape the "petals".

Spiral ribbon

Looking like a twirling Spanish dancer, this unusual design is full of movement. Use a starched napkin that will hold the shape well. The final shaping of the top section is tricky and takes practice.

1 Arrange the open napkin in a square and concertina-pleat it into sixteenths, starting at the lower edge.

2 Tightly roll the strip to approximately two thirds of the way along, then stand the roll upright on the table, making sure the unrolled section of the napkin is right side up.

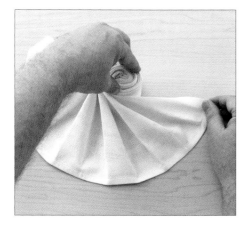

3 ◁ Allow the unrolled material to fan out, guiding it round to form the "skirt".

4 ▷ Holding the coil, turn the napkin over and tuck the loose end into one of the pleats. Turn the napkin back and take hold of the corner at the centre of the coil; very carefully tease it upward and outward to form the "body" of the figure.

Palm leaf

Napkin rings don't have to sit around the middle of napkins. In this arrangement a chunky ring acts as a container for a dramatic large leaf design. An extra fold at the base helps to support the folds, but a sturdy starched napkin is required to maintain the vertical pleats.

1 Fold the napkin diagonally, with the folded edge nearest you.

2 Fold the right-hand corner upward at a slight angle, starting a little away from the centre. Repeat on the other side.

3 Fold the lower edge upward to create a slender band at the base.

4 Make six vertical concertina pleats in the napkin. Slide into a napkin ring and allow the top portion to fall open naturally.

Morning sun

Ideal for a weekend breakfast, this small fan represents the rays of the rising sun. An unpleated section at the back acts as a support to keep the pleats together and helps the folded napkin to stand up.

1 Fold the bottom third of the napkin up and then fold the top third down over the first fold.

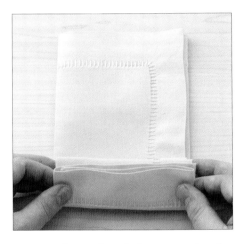

2 Turn the napkin 90 degrees and make eight even concertina pleats from one short end, leaving the final 5cm/2in of the strip unfolded.

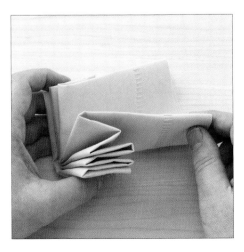

3 ◁ Turn the napkin over and fold it in half so that the pleats are on the outside.

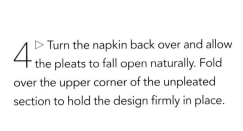

4 ▷ Turn the napkin back over and allow the pleats to fall open naturally. Fold over the upper corner of the unpleated section to hold the design firmly in place.

Double fan

This classic design is ideal for formal dinners. It is satisfying to accomplish but needs a little time to practise it. You will need large starched cotton napkins for the best effect.

1 With the open napkin horizontal and right side down, begin by folding both upper and lower edges to the centre.

2 Fold the napkin in half again by bringing the bottom folded edge up to meet the top.

3 Rotate the napkin so it is arranged vertically. Make eight even concertina pleats.

4 Make sure the double edge is at the top. Holding the fan together at the bottom with one hand, pull down the single edge inside each pleat to make triangular inversions.

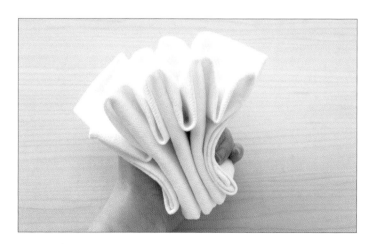

5 Fold down the loose corners at each end to align with the folded edges behind.

6 Turn the napkin around and repeat step 4 on the other side, again folding down the edge inside each pleat.

7 When all the folds have been made the triangular "tucks" on each side should be staggered, creating a zigzag effect.

8 Allow the pleats to open at the top so that the ends fall to the table, keeping the bottom tightly pinched together.

Fanned bow

The fanned bow is perfect for festive occasions, especially if you use a highly decorative napkin ring or a sparkling ribbon tie to secure the centre. The circular shape is perfect on large dinner plates.

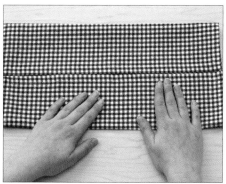

1 Arrange the napkin horizontally, right side down, and fold in the upper and lower edges to meet at the centre.

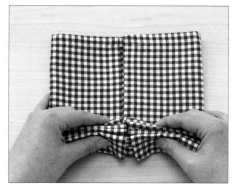

2 Rotate the napkin so that the short end of the rectangle is nearest you, and fold it into 12 even concertina pleats. Press the pleats firmly.

3 Secure the centre of the napkin with narrow ribbon or push a napkin ring into the centre. Fan out the pleats to make a circular shape.

Spreading fan

This elegant, simple design is suitable for all occasions. It is a very pretty way to arrange a napkin with a decorative hem, as the pleats draw attention to a continuous design such as cutwork or embroidery.

1 Arrange the napkin square, right side down, and fold the left-hand side over to the right so that the hemmed edge finishes a little short of the other side. This means both hems will be visible.

2 Make even concertina pleats in the napkin from bottom to top.

3 Clasping the fan together at the centre, slip a napkin ring or a similar fastener around the lower half of the pleats to secure in place.

Springtime

For this rather complex design you will need a large fabric napkin that will hold a crease. A contrasting border or decorative hem will add definition to the tumbling shapes of the pleats.

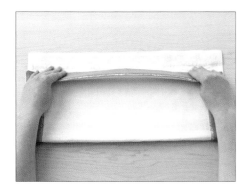

1 Fold the napkin in half horizontally, with the fold at the bottom. Lift the nearer edge of the top layer and make concertina pleats all the way to the fold.

2 Grasp the pleats firmly and turn the napkin over with the pleats nearest you. Holding the centre point, fold up the two sides so that the edges of the pleats meet vertically in the centre.

3 Carefully turn the napkin over again from top to bottom.

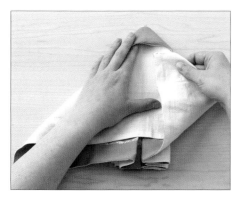

4 Fold the bottom right and left corners up to the top point, tucking them into the pocket created by the pleats.

5 Fold the napkin in half, bringing the top point down to the bottom.

6 Fold the top point away from you again, so that it extends only slightly beyond the top edge.

7 Fold each side corner in toward the centre, and tuck one inside the other.

8 Turn the napkin over carefully and fan out the pleats to create the final shape.

Parasol

Both plain and patterned napkins are appropriate for this attractive design. You will also need a napkin ring or a short length of contrasting ribbon for each napkin to hold the pleats in place.

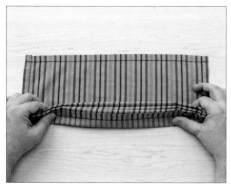

1 With the napkin open and right side up, make concertina pleats from the bottom edge to the top, folding the napkin into sixteenths.

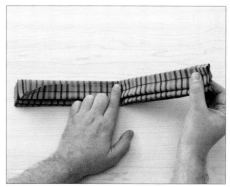

2 Holding a finger firmly at the centre carefully fold the pleated napkin in half from side to side.

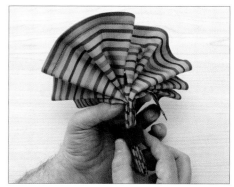

3 Slide a napkin ring half way up the pleats and then fan out the top to make the parasol.

Knotted ribbon

The central knot of this design can be quite bulky because of the number of concertina folds, so use napkins in a fine, crisp fabric about 35cm/14in square. Paper is not really suitable as it may tear.

1 Press the napkin flat and lay it out square. Beginning at the edge nearest to you, pleat the napkin horizontally into sixteenths, pinch-pressing each fold as you make it.

2 Holding the napkin tightly to keep the pleats together, carefully tie the central part into a single knot.

3 ◁ Pull the knot closed but leave it fairly loose so that a guest can undo it easily to use the napkin. It will take some practice to ensure that the finished knot is perfectly central.

4 ▷ Pull out the ends of the pleats into a fan shape.

The fan

Use a carefully starched linen napkin for this classic fold, which can be used for any kind of occasion. It is cleverly designed so that it sits upright securely without any support.

1 Press the napkin flat and lay square, right side down. Fold it horizontally from bottom to top.

2 Fold the left side over to the right to fold the napkin into quarters.

3 Unfold step 2, and align the left-hand edge with the central crease you have just made. Make a firm crease.

4 Pull the vertical edge at the centre back across to the right, so that the napkin is again folded in quarters.

5 Take hold of the sharp crease made in step 3, slide it back towards the left and lay it over the left-hand edge, thus creating a pleat.

6 Fold the same edge back to the left, aligning it with the left-hand edge, making a further pleat.

7 Turn the napkin over bottom to top, keeping the pleated portion on the left, and carefully fold it in half horizontally, so that the pleats appear on the outside.

8 Fold the upper edges of the unpleated right-hand portion down at 45 degrees so that the edges align with the pleats.

9 Fold the excess material at the base (a small rectangle) back underneath the triangular section. This helps to stabilize the form of the finished design.

10 Lift the triangular section until it stands upright from the remaining material. The fan will also rise to a vertical position. Allow the pleats to splay apart naturally.

Fire

This is a spectacular fold that does justice to any special occasion. Using napkins in orange or red it lives up to its name and makes a striking choice for a dinner party, while in pure white or cream the fold takes on a sophisticated flower-like look, perfect for a wedding.

1 Begin with the napkin folded into quarters, arranged as a diamond with the four free corners at the bottom.

2 Fold the upper two layers of the napkin up, matching the corners to the top point of the diamond.

3 Turn the napkin over and repeat with the other two layers on the reverse side to form a triangle.

4 Fold the right-hand half of the triangle across to the left.

5 Fold the same point back to the right by a third of its length, so that one third protrudes beyond the centre fold.

6 Now fold the same point back to the left again, so the upper section is pleated into thirds.

7 Turn the napkin over, keeping it the same way up, and repeat the lateral folds with the triangle on the reverse side.

8 Tightly holding the lower half, tease and spread the points at the top to create the flames. Arrange the napkin in a glass.

Double jabot

The stately double jabot makes an elegant statement on the smartest of tables, but for all its sophistication it is not difficult to do, so it is a viable option for folding in quantity for large formal occasions. Stunning in white double damask, this fold also looks good in strong colours.

1 Fold the napkin into quarters, and arrange as a square with the open corners at the top right.

2 Fold the top layer of fabric diagonally from top right to bottom left, aligning the hems with the folded edges.

3 Fold this triangular flap back on itself by one quarter of its length, parallel with the first diagonal fold.

4 Make two further concertina pleats in the top layer, so that the corner of the napkin finishes at the centre.

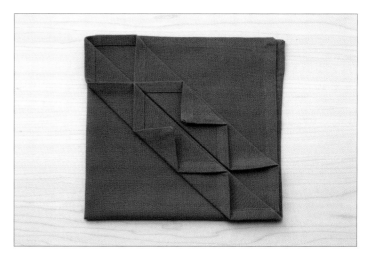

5 Rotate the napkin and repeat the concertina folds in the opposite direction with the second layer.

6 Fold the napkin in half along a diagonal from bottom left to top right, keeping the zigzag pattern on the outside.

7 Bring the two sharp points together and tuck one inside the other. Turn the napkin around to place on the table.

Diamond breeze

This charming informal napkin fold is great for displaying impeccably stitched hems, and combines crisp corners and sculptural lines with a softly draped effect.

1 Press the napkin flat then fold into quarters, with right side out, and arrange in a diamond shape with the open corners at the bottom.

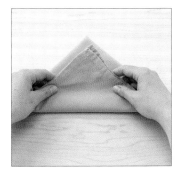

2 Fold the napkin in half diagonally from top to bottom to form a triangle.

3 Turn back the top layer, making the fold close to the long bottom edge of the triangle. Repeat with the second layer, placing it a little further back.

4 Repeat with the remaining layers, keeping the spacing between the hems even and the folds soft.

Scallop

This layered arrangement is given an interesting three-dimensional quality by creating a small tuck at the top that supports the scalloped edges. It looks delicate and pretty in white damask.

1 Fold the napkin into quarters and arrange in a diamond with the four open corners at the top. Fold down the first layer leaving a slender border along the lower edges.

2 Repeat with the three other layers, leaving equal spaces between the hems.

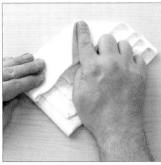

3 Holding the centre point of the upper edge, fold the left side down so that the top edge lies along the vertical centre line. Fold down the right side to match it.

4 Fold back the top point to about halfway down the centre line. Holding it under the napkin, open out the side flaps in soft curves to create scalloped edges.

Chevrons

Made with neatly hemmed and crisply starched plain linen napkins, this design stands with military precision. It adds height to the table and looks smartest with plain, modern china and glassware.

1 Begin with the napkin folded into quarters and with all the open corners at the bottom.

2 Fold the single layer at the bottom up toward the top, leaving a slender border along the upper edges.

3 Fold the second layer up, leaving a border around the edge of the same width as for the first layer.

4 Fold up the third corner, again creating an equal border around the hemmed edges.

5 Repeat with the last layer. Turn the napkin over keeping it the same way up and holding all the layers in place.

6 Roll the triangle around your hand into a cylinder, tucking the corner from one side into one of the folds on the other side.

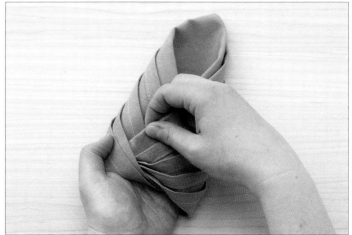

7 Check the alignment of all the layers, then turn the napkin around to stand on the table.

Cream horn

This shape works well with any type of napkin, but for the best effect use it for those with a fairly loose weave and a soft feel. It makes a compact shape suitable for placing on small plates.

1 Begin with the napkin folded into quarters and arranged in a diamond with the four open corners at the bottom. Pick up the first layer and fold it back so that the hemmed edge sits below the upper folded edges.

2 Repeat with the next two layers, leaving equal spaces between the hems.

3 Turn up just a small amount of the final layer so that the lower edge is quite short. Holding all the layers in place, turn the napkin over, keeping the open corners pointing away from you.

4 Holding the centre of the lower edge, curl the sides in so that they meet in the centre. Turn the napkin over to arrange on the plate.

Spear

Though small and neat, this spearhead design makes a strong statement. It shows off the beautiful texture of crisp linen and its sharp angles look best in a minimalist, contemporary setting. It's important to make sure the hems are accurately spaced as attention is focused on them.

1 Fold the napkin into quarters and arrange in a diamond with the open corners at the bottom. Fold back one layer, aligning it with the upper edge.

2 Fold back the remaining layers, staggering the hems evenly.

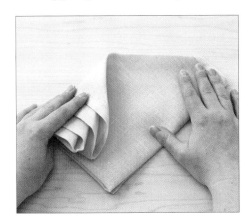

3 Carefully turn the napkin over from top to bottom. Fold in the sides so that the folded edges meet vertically in the centre.

Flowerbud

This charming upstanding design has a fresh, graceful appearance, suitable for a summer lunch party. It is an ideal design for good-quality paper napkins as well as patterned or figured fabric.

1 Fold the napkin in half diagonally, right side out, and fold the top corner down to the bottom to create a triangle.

2 From the centre of the long edge, fold the left-hand sharp point down to the right-angled corner and repeat with the right-hand side so that the edges meet vertically in the centre.

3 Fold the bottom half of the resulting diamond shape up to the top to make a triangle.

4 Fold the two uppermost layers down toward you, so that about half the point protrudes below the lower edge.

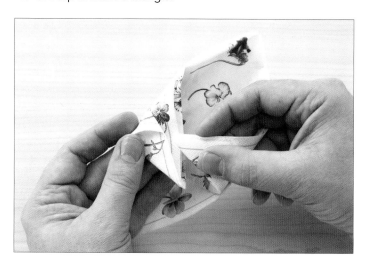

5 Turn the napkin over and roll into a cylinder around your hand, tucking one sharp corner into the pocket of the other.

6 Turn the napkin around and tuck the lower flap up inside the cylinder to help hold the folds in place.

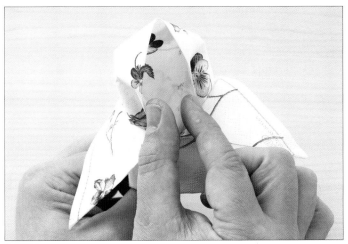

7 Holding the lower section, pull down the two loose points from the top to form "petals".

8 Shape the "bud" at the centre by opening out the front slit and rounding the sides to give the desired effect.

Tulip

Chunky linen napkins with an interesting texture will give substance to this lovely simple design. It is easier to manipulate the folds to give a shapely result when using soft, pliable fabric.

1 Begin by folding the napkin in half diagonally, folding the bottom corner up to the top.

2 Fold both layers of the top corner down so that they touch the centre of the lower edge.

3 From the centre of the lower edge, fold the right-hand side across at an angle of about 30 degrees from the vertical.

4 Repeat with the left-hand side, so that the two sections overlap with the sharp points at the same height.

5 Holding the previous folds, turn the napkin over from top to bottom.

6 Fold up the two lower points, pulling them apart slightly.

7 Shape the bloom by folding the outer edges back at the desired angle.

Cicada

This innovative design is ideal for printed paper napkins, as its effectiveness is enhanced by the unprinted wrong side appearing as a panel across the centre of the insect.

1 Arrange the open napkin, right side down, as a diamond and fold the bottom half over the top to form a triangle.

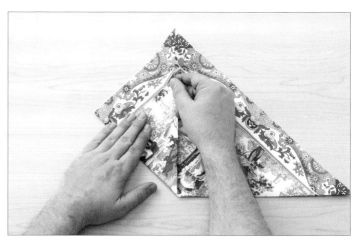

2 From the centre of the long bottom edge, fold the sharp corners at left and right up to the right-angled top corner.

3 Fold these corners back down at a slight angle, creating a space between the central point and each of the "wings".

4 Fold down the single layer so that the corner comes just above the central point. The wrong side will be visible.

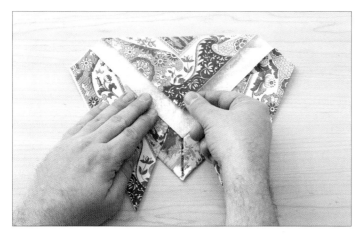

5 Fold down the remaining layer to a higher point, creating a V-shaped panel across the body.

6 Turn the napkin over and fold the sides inward at an angle to shape the body. Turn the napkin over to place on the table.

French lily

A charming traditional fold, the French lily is reminiscent of the heraldic fleur-de-lys, with its historic associations. Choose large, starched napkins for this one, as they help to keep the lily in shape.

1 Arrange the napkin in a diamond and fold the bottom corner up to the top corner to form a triangle.

2 Fold the two sharp points up to the right-angled corner so that the folded edges meet vertically in the centre.

3 Turn up the lower corner to approximately three-quarters of the way up the middle of the napkin.

4 Turn the upper part of the previous fold back down toward you so that the point touches the lower edge.

5 Turn the napkin over and roll it into a cylinder around your hand, overlapping the two outer corners.

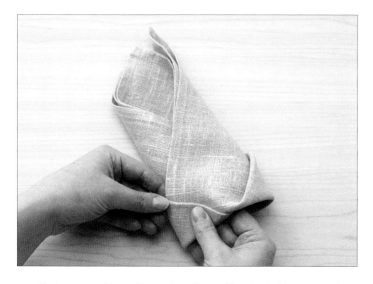

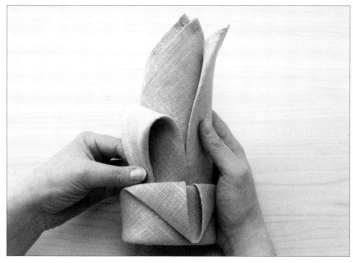

6 Tuck one end into the pocket formed by the folds in the other end, to hold the napkin together.

7 Turn the napkin around and curl down the loose flaps at either side, tucking the points inside the lower pocket.

Napkins for
special events

Festive meals, children's celebrations and family

birthdays and anniversaries all deserve their own special

table settings, and this section contains some really

novel and creative napkin designs to amuse and delight

guests of all ages.

Heart

A heart on a plate conveys an unmistakable romantic message for an intimate dinner. This is an easy shape to make but needs to be folded with precision and requires napkins that will hold creases well, so choose crisp linen – in pink or red, of course.

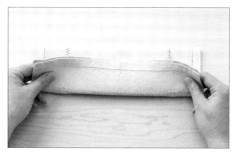

1 Fold the napkin in half, bringing the top edge down to meet the bottom edge. Fold almost in half again, bringing the bottom edge up just short of the top.

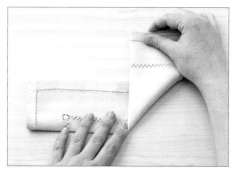

2 Holding the centre point of the bottom edge of the napkin, fold the right-hand side up vertically.

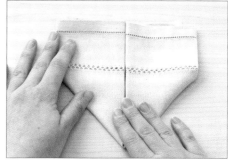

3 Repeat with the left side, creating a sharp point at the base of the heart.

4 Shape the top of the heart by folding the four top corners underneath.

The knot

This is a very simple, unstructured design, but you can load it with symbolism when it's used to decorate the table for a romantic candlelit dinner, or an anniversary breakfast. It takes a little practice and a confident hand to make a casual-looking yet stylish shape.

1 Arrange the open napkin in the form of a diamond, with right side down, and fold the bottom point up to the top to make a triangle.

2 Starting from the long edge, make concertina pleats up to the point.

3 With the pleats facing away from you, fold the right point over the left and tuck back through the loop created to form a loose but tidy knot.

Valentine rose

In this wonderful flight of fancy, an ordinary paper napkin turns into a very realistic-looking rose. It's unlikely that you or your guest will want to dismantle it, so provide more napkins for the meal.

1 Begin with the napkin opened out completely and arranged as a square.

2 Fold over the left-hand vertical edge to create a border. Many paper napkins have a perforated design that can act as a guide.

3 Fold up the lower edge to make a matching border along the bottom.

4 Place two fingers at the lower left corner, pointing inward, and grasp this corner. Take hold of the top of the napkin with your right hand.

5 Wrap the napkin over and around your fingers, with the aiming of creating a neat cylindrical roll.

6 Once you have a slender tube, pinch it together about 5cm/2in from the top; the top part will form the bud.

7 Roll the stem tightly from the bud down, taking care not to tear the paper. Stop halfway down.

8 Take hold of the loose corner at the base of the stem and start teasing it up toward the bud.

9 Gradually pull out the excess paper a little at a time, straightening the stem as necessary before continuing.

10 The corner of the flap will become the leaf. Below it, continue twisting the stem tightly to the bottom, then shape the leaf.

11 For a fuller bloom with more inner petals, take hold of the corner of the paper in the middle of the bud and twist to tighten the spiral.

12 Curl the upper edges of the petals, creating a very fine border, to define the form of the flower when viewed from the side.

Easter bunny

These perky bunny ears are the perfect greeting for young partygoers arriving at the table – and they're especially appropriate at Easter. The brighter the napkins you choose for this design, the better.

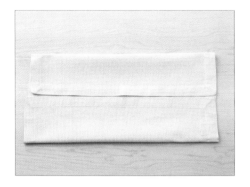

1 Fold both the upper and lower edges of the napkin to the centre.

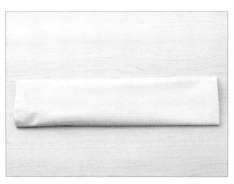

2 Fold the napkin in half by bringing the bottom edge up to the top edge.

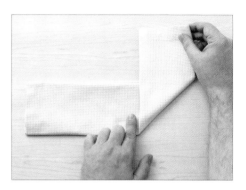

3 Fold the right-hand side of the napkin up from the centre point so that the folded edge is vertical.

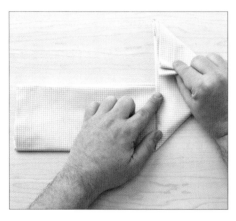

4 Fold both layers of the top right-hand corner diagonally down to the centre.

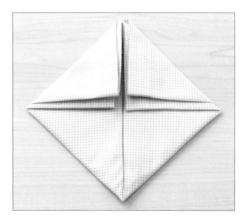

5 Repeat the last two steps on the left-hand side to form a diamond shape.

6 Fold the right-hand upper edge down to the vertical centre line and repeat with the left-hand upper edge.

7 Holding the folds in place, fold the bottom point up underneath, forming a triangle.

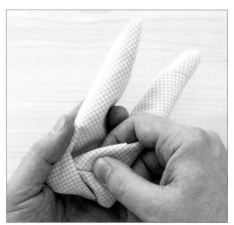

8 Take the bottom corner on one side across and tuck it into the pocket on the other side to form the base. Round out the shape of the base from underneath using your finger.

9 Turn the napkin round and shape the head by opening out and rounding the small "pouch" beneath the ears.

Coronet

A stately crown in starched white damask at each place setting looks dignified for a formal occasion, but you could also use this design in rich festive colours to complete a Christmas table.

1 Arrange the open napkin as a square, right side down, and fold it horizontally into thirds.

2 Fold each short edge in to lie a short distance from the centre, leaving a gap.

3 Fold the bottom left and top right corners in at 45 degrees so that the edges meet along the vertical centre line.

4 Turn the napkin over and rotate it so that a diagonal edge is at the bottom. Fold the upper edge down to the lower edge, allowing the loose corners to flip out.

5 All four points should now be positioned at the top. Tuck the right-hand point between the two diagonals at the left-hand side.

6 Turn the napkin over and repeat, tucking the other end into the fold behind the front triangle.

7 Shape the design by carefully opening out the base to separate the two sides and rounding out the top.

The swan

Although the swan can be made from stiff fabric, thin paper napkins work better. If you wish, you can slide the chest of the swan between the prongs of an upturned fork, which can then be placed across the plate to hold the napkin in place. The design is free-standing, however.

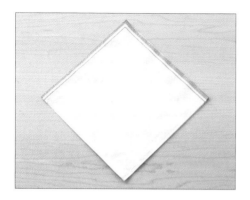

1 Keeping the napkin folded into quarters, arrange it as a diamond with an open corner at the top. Fold it in half vertically to establish the vertical diagonal, then unfold it.

2 Fold the right-hand corner to the vertical centre line and repeat on the left to form a kite shape.

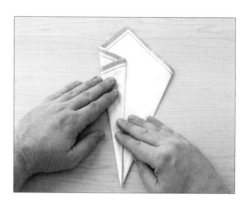

3 Turn the napkin over keeping the sharp point nearest you and the open corners at the top. Fold in the left-hand outer edge to the centre, holding the napkin firmly to stop the layers unfolding.

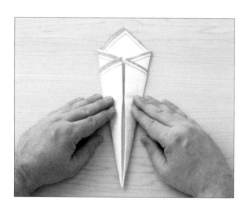

4 Fold in the right-hand outer edge to the vertical centre line to match the previous fold.

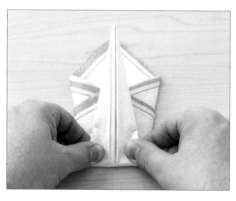

5 Fold the napkin in half, taking the sharp point at the bottom up to the top.

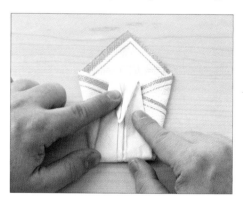

6 Fold approximately one-third of the sharp point back down toward you to create the head of the swan.

7 Fold the napkin in half lengthwise, bending the sides back. The neck and head flaps should finish on the outside.

8 Hold the napkin firmly along the lower edge of the body with one hand.

9 Lift the neck away from the body and flatten the base to keep it in place. Lift and flatten the head. Gently pull up the layers to form the body of the swan.

The corsage

For this attractive flower-like design a small and a large napkin are folded as one. This would be a nice arrangement for a meal in which paper napkins are needed for a first course eaten with the fingers.

1 Place a small napkin on top of a larger one, so that there is a border of equal width all round the edge. Arrange as a diamond.

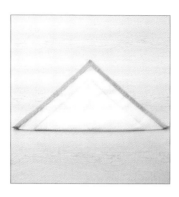

2 Carefully fold both napkins in half diagonally as one, right sides together, with the smaller of the two napkins on the inside.

3 Fold the napkin carefully into quarters.

4 Lift the top triangle to a vertical position and allow it to open out symmetrically, rotating the napkin so the open edges are nearest you.

5 Begin squashing the upper folded edge down, and flatten the section to form a diamond shape.

6 Turn the napkin over and repeat the last two steps on the reverse side.

7 Beginning at the closed corner, turn in the folded edge of the top layer, aligning it with the centre line.

8 Repeat on the other side of the top layer, then turn the napkin over and repeat on the other side.

9 Fold the sharp point over at right angles to the central line to touch the edges of the triangular flaps created in steps 7 and 8.

10 Fold the napkin tightly in half along its length. Turn the napkin over. Holding the closed end firmly with one hand, start to tease out the four corners.

11 Spread out the four petals to shape the flower and reveal the inner napkin at the centre.

Candle fan

This neat, symmetrically pleated and rolled arrangement is designed to be inserted in a glass and calls for stiffly starched fabric napkins with a fine, firm weave that will hold the creases well, or thick paper.

1 Press the napkin flat and arrange it in a square, right side down. Fold in the left and right outer edges to meet vertically at the centre.

2 Find the centre point and peel back the lower left-hand flap as far as it will comfortably go, making the crease from the centre to the bottom left-hand corner.

3 Repeat with the remaining three corners, so that the two sides of the napkin meet at the centre point only.

4 Starting at the bottom edge, make six or eight concertina pleats to the horizontal centre line.

5 Use a paperclip to keep this pleated section together while you are working on the remaining half of the napkin.

6 Rotate the napkin by 180 degrees and form the candles by rolling the lower edge up to the centre.

7 Remove the paperclip from the pleated side, and with the rolled section on top, carefully fold the napkin in half lengthwise, bringing the two ends of the roll together.

8 Push the folded centre of the napkin into a glass, allowing the rolls to splay apart a little and the pleats to open to produce the desired shape.

Butterfly

This pleated design looks pretty made with delicately coloured and patterned paper napkins, creating a collection of butterflies to settle lightly on your table for a summer lunch party.

1 Arrange the napkin in a square and make concertina pleats from the bottom edge, dividing the lower half into eighths. The centre line of the napkin should be used to form the final pleat.

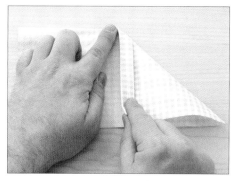

2 Turn the napkin over so that the pleated portion lies underneath at the top, and the shape is a rectangle. Fold the top right-hand corner down at 45 degrees so that the edges of the pleats align with the central vertical line.

3 Fold the top left-hand corner down at 45 degrees to match the other side and form a triangle.

4 Turn the napkin over from side to side and fold the top point down to the lower edge.

5 Fold this point back up again so that its tip (the head of the butterfly) protrudes above the body.

6 Fold the right-hand sharp point up so that the lower edge lies along the vertical centre line.

7 Fold this triangle back down so that the point touches the lower edge.

8 Fold the right-hand half of the napkin, including all the layers, across to the left along the central vertical line.

9 Fold the left-hand corner to the centre, aligning the lower edges.

10 Fold this small triangular section upward and tuck it into the pocket created in what was the right-hand side.

11 Turn the napkin over and spread the wings. The design is supported by the triangular section under the body.

The duck

An inventive design to appeal to cartoon fans of all ages, this impressionistic version of the hot-tempered Donald Duck glowers up from under his rakishly tilted peaked cap.

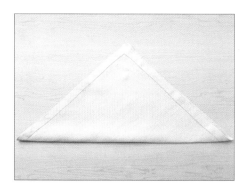

1 Press the napkin flat and arrange in a diamond. Fold it in half diagonally, taking the bottom corner to the top, to make a triangle.

2 Fold up a slender border along the lower edge of the triangle.

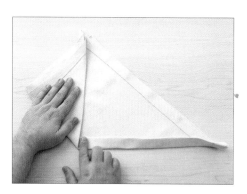

3 Find the centre of the lower edge and fold up the left-hand side a little away from that point. Repeat with the right-hand side so the points meet at the top.

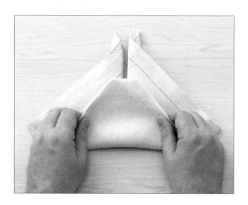

4 Fold the lower edge approximately three-quarters of the way up the vertical centre line.

5 Double this short edge back down to the bottom of the napkin, creating a pleat, as shown.

6 Turn the napkin over and roll into a cylinder, tucking one side into the diagonal folds created in the other side.

7 Curl over the loose points at the top to create eyes; tuck the ends inside the pleated section below to secure.

8 Fold the top points over and shape to suggest the duck's peaked cap.

Turbo

Designed to stand in a tall glass and very easy and quick to do, this napkin is meant to loosely represent a space rocket, so it would be a good choice for a child's birthday party table. Use paper napkins with bold, brightly coloured motifs.

1 Fold the napkin in half with the fold along the top edge.

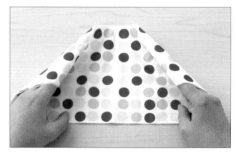

2 Hold one of the top corners tightly in each hand and carefully roll the napkin in from each corner over your fingers.

3 As the rolls get closer to the centre you may need to turn the napkin in your hands so that you don't let go of it.

4 Try to keep the two rolls even. When you reach the centre, place the napkin point down in a glass to hold the shape.

The dog

This is an ideal design for small children, and would work well with either fabric or paper napkins. A few small candies are used to make the eyes and nose as a winning finishing touch.

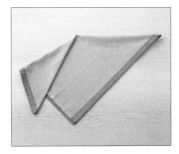

1 Arrange the napkin as a diamond with right side down. Fold the top half down, aligning the edges, to make a triangle. Find the centre of the long edge, and from that point fold the left-hand side down at about 30 degrees.

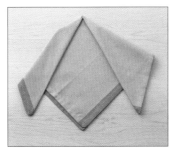

2 Fold the right-hand side down at the same angle to form the ears. Turn under about one-third of the folds along each sloping side.

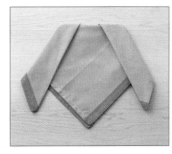

3 Turn under the top point of the napkin to form the top of the dog's head.

4 Turn up both layers of the bottom corners to form the dog's snout. Arrange a candy nose centrally at the top of this flap and add the two eyes.

GI cap

Always popular with children, this little hat will inevitably start off on the heads of young guests rather than in their laps. It looks best in crisp linen in deep colours such as navy or green.

1 With the napkin arranged as a square, right side down, fold the top edge down to the bottom edge, then fold in the left and right edges of the rectangle to meet in the centre.

2 Take hold of the inner loose corner of the right-hand portion and peel open the single layer of material to the right, while holding the second layer in place. As you do this allow the upper section to flatten into a triangle. Repeat with the top layer of fabric on the left.

3 ◁ Turn the napkin over and fold in both outer edges to the centre.

4 ▷ Fold the single layer at the bottom up to the horizontal centre line, then double this portion over again. Turn the napkin over and repeat on the remaining side. Open out the napkin so that it stands freely with the folded edge along the top. Use your thumb to dimple this edge.

Flame

Make this uncomplicated shape using beautifully textured and hemmed linen napkins in rich, deep tones to add a series of stately vertical forms to a sophisticated table setting.

1 Begin by folding the napkin into quarters, right side out, and arrange as a diamond with the open corners nearest you at the bottom.

2 Fold a single layer from the bottom corner upward, leaving a slender border along the upper edges.

3 ◁ Repeat with the remaining layers of the napkin, staggering the edges equally beneath the preceding layers.

4 ▷ Turn the napkin over and roll it into a cylinder, tucking the corner of one side in between the layers of the other.

Samurai helmet

The traditional origami design for a model of a Japanese warrior's helmet translates very effectively into a fold for fabric or paper napkins, creating a pleasingly detailed symmetrical form.

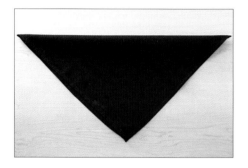

1 Arrange the open napkin as a diamond and fold it in half diagonally, taking the top corner to the bottom.

2 From the centre of the long top edge, fold each of the sharp points of the triangle down to the right-angled corner, forming a diamond.

3 Fold the two sharp points back up to the top corner.

4 Fold each sharp point outward so that the folded edge is at right angles to the long sloping edge, to form the "wings".

5 Pick up a single layer at the lower corner and fold it upward so that the point is about halfway up the upper triangle.

6 Double over the portion of this layer below the central horizontal fold to create a "brim" across the base.

7 Turn the napkin over and fold the remaining layer at the lower edge all the way up behind to form the back of the helmet.

Mr Spoon

This ingenious design has a spoon slotted into its folds, which forms the head of a little man lying in each plate ready to join in the fun of a party meal. It will delight children and grown-ups alike.

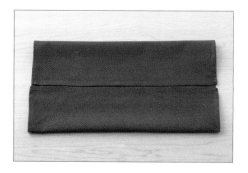

1 Open out the napkin and arrange as a square, with right side down. Fold in the upper and lower edges so that they meet at the horizontal centre line.

2 Find the centre point and open out each of the four corners diagonally from that point.

3 Beginning with the left-hand side, carefully roll the napkin up to the vertical centre line.

4 Roll up the right side to match. (You may want to pin the first roll in place while working on the other side.)

5 Fold back the upper section of the rolls to form the arms of the little man.

6 Turn the napkin over, and carefully pull the arms apart (this is easier with a fabric napkin) to give the desired effect.

7 Slide the handle of a spoon down inside the layers of the body leaving the bowl protruding to form the head.

Ocean liner

A fleet of these sturdy-looking little ships in brightly coloured paper napkins would be just right for a summer party with a nautical theme, or even for a celebratory picnic at the seaside.

1 Leave the paper napkin folded in quarters and arrange in a diamond with the open corners at the bottom. Fold in half diagonally, bringing the top of the napkin down over the bottom.

2 Rotate the napkin so that the right-angled corner is at the bottom left, then fold up the lower edge to form the hull, making the fold deeper towards the right-hand side.

3 Open out the lower fold and turn the open layers of the hull out and up the other side to enfold the remaining triangular portion of the napkin.

4 Fold the upper triangle down parallel with the hull, then fold it back up and down again once more.

5 Fold the point of the triangle up again. These random pleats will form the cabin and the funnel of the ship.

6 Unfold the concertina pleats made in steps 4 and 5. Open out the diagonal crease of the large triangular portion.

7 Using the creases made in steps 4 and 5, fold the upper corner down and up along the central diagonal.

8 Fold the tip of the upper corner over toward the front of the ship and double it over again to make the funnel.

9 At the open back end of the ship turn in a short vertical fold on each side through all the layers.

10 Interlock the pleats in the open ends. Open out the underside of the hull a little so that the ship stands up.

Fish

A streamlined fish with gracefully folded fins and tail is an appropriate idea for a party table with a seaside feel. A single candy eye transforms an almost abstract fold into a creature with personality.

1 Arrange the open napkin in a square, right side up. Fold over the left-hand edge to make a narrow border.

2 Fold the napkin in half horizontally so that the fold at the left-hand side is on the outside.

3 Pick up the top right-hand corner and fold it down at 45 degrees so that the right-hand side of the napkin aligns with the lower edge. Crease then open the fold.

4 Pick up the top layer at the right-hand side, forming the diagonal crease with the layers below. Refold the top layer.

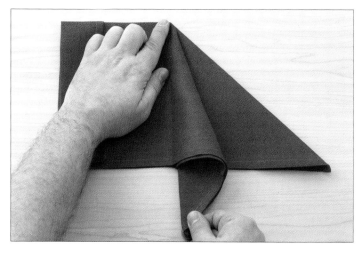

5 Pick up the top layer of the triangular section and fold it under from the top so that the folded edge is vertical.

6 Fold the lower layer to match the previous fold, turning it in the opposite direction.

7 Fold the bottom layer upward, aligning the crease with the tip of the fish's head to form the tail fin.

8 Rotate the napkin slightly so the fish is horizontal and fold up the lower section of the top layer of the body.

9 Fold up the lower section at a shallower angle to complete the fin. Lay the fish on a plate and position the eye.

Christmas tree

This classic fold for a traditional Christmas table is very simple and quick to do but has a satisfying three-dimensional quality, suggesting not only a stylized Christmas tree but also a four-pointed star.

1 Fold the napkin in quarters and arrange it as a square with the open corners at the bottom. Fold in half, bringing the top edge down to the bottom edge.

2 Take hold of the top layer by the lower right-hand corner and slide it over to the lower left corner, allowing the napkin to flatten into a triangular shape. With a paper napkin the vertical centre crease will help this procedure.

3 Turn the napkin over from side to side, keeping it the same way up, and repeat step 2 on the reverse side, creating a triangle.

4 Fold the triangle in half from side to side to create the inner vertical creases, then spread out the branches of the tree vertically and stand up on the table.

Christmas candle

A festive fold based on a universal seasonal symbol is perfect for Christmas. Green or red napkins would be particularly suitable, and a decorative border creates a stylish diagonal accent.

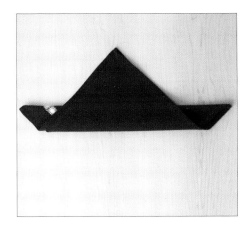

1 Arrange the open napkin as a diamond, right side down, and fold the bottom corner up to the top. Fold the lower edge up to form a narrow border, then turn the napkin over.

2 Rotate the napkin through 90 degrees so that the long folded edge is on the left. Roll up the napkin, beginning from the bottom point and stopping short of the small top tail.

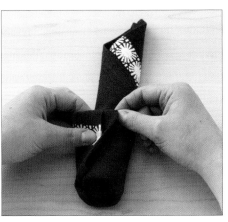

3 ◁ Turn the candle round so that the tail is facing you and tuck it into the band around the base to secure the roll.

4 ▷ Tuck the free corner at the top down into the roll and form a flame shape with the second free corner underneath.

Christmas stocking

This jolly Christmas stocking will add some festive cheer to your party table – you could even hide a little extra gift inside, or arrange a candy cane sticking out of the top to complete the picture.

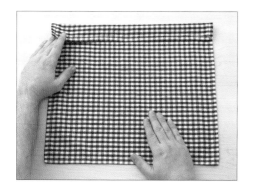

1 Arrange the napkin in a square, right side down, and fold over a narrow border along the upper edge.

2 Turn the napkin over from side to side so that the folded border lies under the upper edge. Fold the two sides in so that the edges meet along the vertical centre line.

3 Fold the two lower corners in at 45 degrees, aligning the sides along the vertical centre line.

4 Fold up the point at the bottom of the napkin so that it meets the centre of the long edge of the triangular section.

5 Holding the lower folds in place, fold the napkin in half from bottom to top.

6 Fold down the upper layer toward you, lining up the corner of the triangle with the right-angle beneath, to create a pleat.

7 Fold the napkin in half vertically. Holding the top section, swing out the excess fabric in the pleat to angle the toe.

Christmas star

This elegant six-pointed star is satisfying to fold and makes a simple statement on an elaborately decorated Christmas table. The flat, symmetrical shape is a perfect fit for circular dinner plates.

1 Arrange the napkin in a square, right side down, and fold it in half, taking the bottom edge to the top.

2 Open out the napkin again, and take the lower right-hand corner to the left, folding from the top right-hand corner, so that it rests on the centre crease.

3 Fold the bottom edge up at the point where the lower right-hand corner and the two upper corners form an equilateral triangle. (This requires experimentation.)

4 Fold the lower left-hand corner across to form the equilateral triangle described in step 3.

5 Fold the top left-hand corner across to the centre of the right-hand side.

6 Fold this point back outward to form a pleat, aligning the crease with the centre of the napkin.

7 Repeat step 6 with the two remaining corners of the triangle to create the six points of the star.

8 To lock the flaps in place, lift up the corner of the last fold and tuck it under the folded edges of its neighbour. Turn over.

Complex folds

Most traditional napkin designs are swift to fold and simple to remember so that you can use them frequently and consistently. The ideas in this section are mostly representational and are a little more elaborate in construction, but one of these could be just what you need for a themed celebration.

The slipper

Winsome fairytale slippers lend a magical touch to a celebration table. Each napkin makes one slipper, but a pair placed on each plate could make the setting even more appealing. A tiny stick-on gem adds a witty finishing touch to this charming napkin fold.

1 Fold the napkin in half, bringing the top edge down to the bottom.

2 Fold the napkin in half again, bringing the top edge down to the bottom.

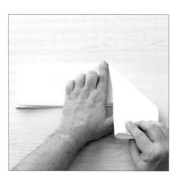

3 Fold down the right-hand side at 45 degrees to lie along the vertical centre line.

4 Fold down the left-hand side in the same way so that the folded edges meet.

5 Narrow the point at the top by folding the sloping side in to lie along the vertical centre line.

6 Fold in the remaining side of the napkin to match.

7 Fold the napkin in half along the vertical centre line and hold the napkin so that the folded edge lies along the top. The smooth pointed triangle will become the toe.

8 Rotate the napkin so that it is horizontal. Fold a single layer of the large flap at the rear upward to lie along the edge of the toe section.

9 Fold the excess triangular flap of the underlying layer forward over the edge as shown, to narrow the portion protruding at the heel.

10 Carefully wrap the excess material around and tuck deep inside the pocket created by the edges of the toe section (the shortest edge of the triangle).

11 Stand the napkin upright, flattening the toe to help this, and shape the vertical section by rounding into a kind of cylinder from above.

Water lily

Using a well-starched napkin, this classic design creates a cup shape that can be used to hold a bread roll or a small gift, a few chocolate hearts for Valentine's Day or a tiny posy of spring flowers.

1 Open out the napkin right side down and fold all four corners to the centre.

2 Fold all four corners of the new square you have created to the centre again.

3 Turn the napkin over, using a hand on either side to keep the flaps in place.

4 Pick up each corner of the new square in turn and fold them into the centre once more.

5 Take hold of the loose double flap under one corner and pull it upward so that the point almost turns inside out; you will need to hold down the rest of the napkin firmly with the other hand in the centre. Repeat with the three other corners.

6 Still holding the centre, tease out from underneath the single loose flap between two of the main petals.

7 Repeat with the remaining flaps to create extra petals or leaves all round the water lily.

Mitre

This classic design epitomizes the art of napkin folding. Smart and majestic, it is best reserved for the most formal of occasions. Despite its grandness, however, it is quite quick to fold.

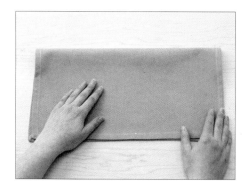

1 Arrange the open napkin as a square, right side down, and fold it in half, bringing the upper edge to meet the lower edge.

2 Fold the top right-hand corner down at 45 degrees to the lower edge, then fold the bottom left-hand corner upward so that the edges meet along the centre line, creating a parallelogram.

3 Holding the folds in place, turn the napkin over and rotate it so that a diagonal edge is at the bottom.

4 Fold the upper edge down to the lower edge, leaving the loose corner beneath unfolded.

5 Pull out the trapped corner of the front triangular section so that both points are at the top.

6 Fold the right-hand side across on a vertical crease down from the right-hand point.

7 Lift up the large triangular front flap and tuck the loose corner from the previous step behind it.

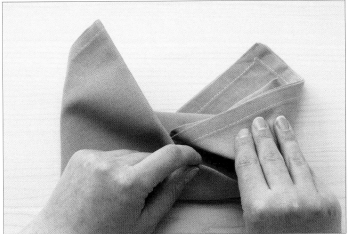

8 Turn the napkin over and repeat, tucking the other end into the fold behind the front triangle.

9 Shape the napkin by carefully opening out the base to separate the two sides and rounding out the centre.

Carousel

Use crisply starched medium-sized napkins for this spectacular design, which produces a three-dimensional sculptural shape with a circular outline that sits perfectly on a dinner plate.

1 Begin with the napkin folded into quarters, with the open corners at the lower left-hand side.

2 Lift up the top layer at the left corner and slide it all the way across to the right, so that the upper folded edge opens and falls over the vertical central line.

3 Turn the napkin over from side to side so that it is still the same way up.

4 Lift up the single layer at the right corner and slide it across to the lower left, again allowing the fabric to flatten.

5 Press the folds on the sloping sides, creating a triangle with the open edges at the base.

6 Lift up the single top layer and fold it upward so that the two corners of the napkin are drawn into the centre.

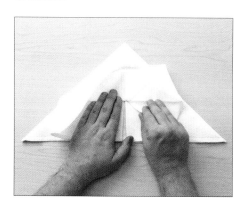

7 You will need to experiment slightly with the position of the fold; the two side corners when flattened should meet in the centre without overlapping.

8 Turn the napkin over and fold up the single layer on the second side to match the first, bringing the other two corners to meet in the centre.

9 Using the vertical centre line as the axis, fold a single layer from the right-hand side across to the left.

10 Fold the lower edge upward, matching the previous folds. Turn the napkin over once more from side to side and repeat steps 8 and 9 on the other side.

11 Stand the napkin upright and fan out the four main flaps to point north, south, east and west, while allowing the inner folds to fall forward to complete the circular outline.

Nautilus shell

This is an ambitious-looking asymmetical design but the shape is mainly created by folding triangles of diminishing size to achieve the spiral effect. Once you have mastered the technique it is quick to do.

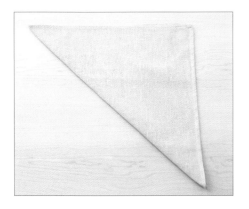

1 Arrange the open napkin as a square, right side down, and fold the lower left corner to the top right to make a triangle.

2 Fold down the top edge so that the two triangles formed on the left and lower right are equal in size.

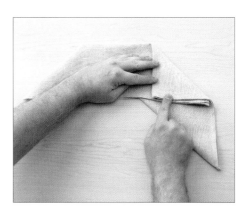

3 Turn in the top right-hand corner at 45 degrees so that the side edge aligns with the edge of the previous fold.

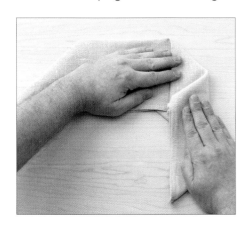

4 Turn in the right-hand side vertically so that it aligns with the edge of the previous fold.

5 Turn in the downward-facing section at 45 degrees, starting the crease in line with the long horizontal edge. Repeat the triangular folds until the end of the section is pointing up.

6 Secure the spiral by tucking the end of the tail section into the previous folds.

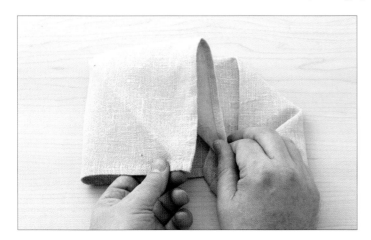

7 Pick up the sharp left-hand corner and take it across between the layers of the left-hand section, aligning the bottom edges.

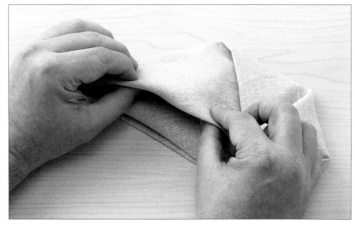

8 Turn in the two triangular sections below the central horizontal line to form the mouth of the shell.

Overcoat

This charming little coat is best made from a paper napkin with a contrasting border design, which will accentuate the clever details such as the sleeves and the stylish narrow lapels. Everyone will love it.

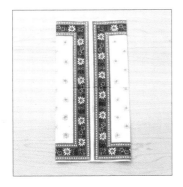

1 Open out the napkin flat. Fold the two vertical edges in to meet at the centre.

2 Turn the napkin over. Turn in a small hem on the same two vertical folds. Press and open out.

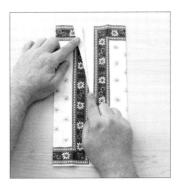

3 Turn the napkin over. Find the centre point along the raw edges. Keeping your finger on this point, turn back a small collar at each side.

4 Fold back and press the top third of the napkin.

5 To form the waist, make a pleat so that the folded edge is a third of the way from the bottom edge of the napkin.

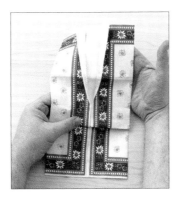

6 Open out the top fold, but keep the lower pleat in place.

7 Refold the vertical folds at each side of the napkin.

8 Now refold the napkin one-third of the way from the top edge.

9 The back edge of the top fold is used to form the sleeves. Tease out the fold at the sides to form arms.

10 To form the shoulders, turn under a small diagonal fold at each top edge.

Pinwheel

This lovely design looks great on a party table, creating a real sense of movement, and will especially appeal to children as it really does look as if it could turn in the breeze.

1 Open the napkin out flat with right side down, and fold the four corners into the centre to form a diamond.

2 Fold two opposite edges inward to meet in the centre, creating a rectangle.

3 Fold the two short edges of the rectangle to meet in the centre, creating a small square.

4 Carefully tease out the loose corners from under the flap nearest you, holding the napkin firmly with the other hand.

5 Flatten the flap to make a point at each end, then swing the right-hand point down towards you; this forms two blades.

6 Turn the napkin round and repeat steps 4 and 5 to form the remaining two blades of the pinwheel.

The shirt

This is a clever design that is really much easier to make up than it looks. Make it with impeccably pressed and starched linen or cotton napkins, either plain or in smart stripes or checks.

1 Arrange the napkin right side down and fold all four corners to the centre.

2 Fold the two side edges of the square in to meet in the centre.

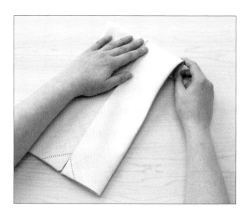

3 At the upper edge, fold a slender strip behind to form the collar.

4 Fold the upper corners in so that they meet at the vertical centre line a short way from the top edge.

5 Fold out the right flap from the lower corner; the angle is not critical but the point should protrude beyond the outer edge.

6 Fold out the left-hand flap from the same point on the vertical centre line. The points of these two flaps form the sleeves.

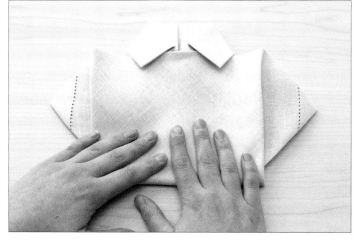

7 Fold up the lower edge and tuck it underneath the points of the collar created in step 4.

Bow tie

For a grand dinner at which the guests are formally dressed, you can match the bow ties of the men
with this snappy design, which is suitable for napkins of a fairly modest size.

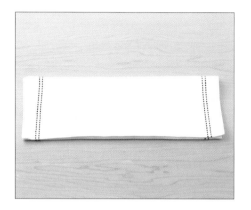

1 Open out the napkin with right side
down and fold it horizontally into
thirds, folding the upper portion down
over the lower portion.

2 Fold the left-hand edge across to the
right-hand edge.

3 At the left-hand, folded edge, fold in
both corners at 45 degrees so that the
edges meet horizontally in the centre.

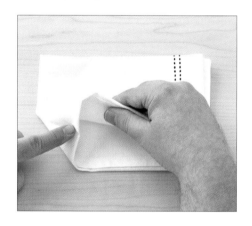

4 Unfold the corners. Lift up the lower
top layer and push the corner in
between the layers along the creases
made previously.

5 Flatten the napkin with the corner now
turned inside. Repeat the process with
the upper corner.

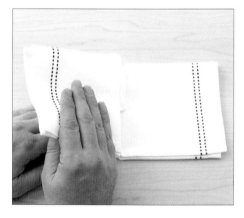

6 Lift up the top half of the napkin at the
right-hand edge, and fold it back to
the left as far as it will go: the crease will
run along the edges of the small tucks.

7 Turn the napkin over and repeat step 6 on the reverse. At the
folded edges, again fold in the outer corners at 45 degrees.

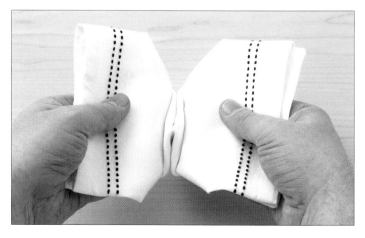

8 Carefully holding the edges and all the folds previously made
at the centre, open out the two large flaps.

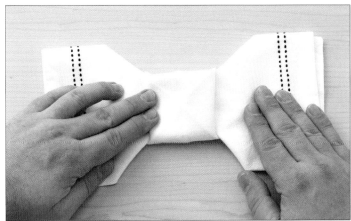

9 Allow the central point to flatten into a square; hold all the corner flaps firmly until this begins to happen.

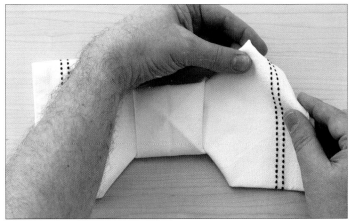

10 Smooth out the central square and shape the napkin by folding the four outer corners back.

Papillon

The brighter and more varied the colours of the napkin you use for this design, the more glamorous will be the butterfly that emerges. Begin with the patterned side of the napkin face down.

1 Arrange the napkin in a square and fold the bottom edge up to the top.

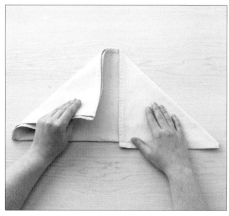

2 Fold both upper corners down at 45 degrees to lie along the centre line.

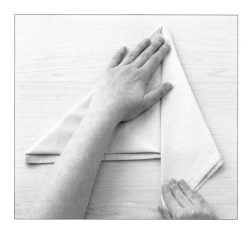

3 Turn the napkin over. Fold the right side in to lie along the centre line.

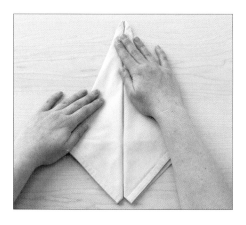

4 Fold in the left-hand side in the same way to meet the first side in the centre.

5 Slide out the loose corner from beneath each side, creating a diamond-shaped outline.

6 Turn the napkin over from side to side so the loose layers are underneath.

7 Fold down the top point and tuck it into the pocket formed by the horizontal edge.

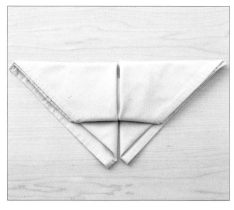

8 Press the fold flat and arrange the butterfly on the plate or table.

9 To create the body, push the wings together to make a narrow pleat at the centre. The upper wing tips should move up slightly while the tips of the tail wings should spread apart a little.

Oriental fold

This eye-catching design with a Japanese feel requires two fabric napkins, which are folded together. One should be larger than the other and for the best effect they should be in contrasting colours.

1 Arrange the small napkin right side down and cover it with the larger napkin, also right side down, making sure the centre points match. Holding both napkins, fold all the corners into the centre.

2 Carefully turn the square over and fold up the bottom third, letting the loose corners straighten out.

3 Fold down the top third, again allowing the loose corners to open out.

4 At each end, tuck the top corners into the triangular flaps beneath them.

The place mat

If you have pretty plates you don't want to hide, or are planning to put the first course on the table before your guests sit down to eat, this fold enables you to arrange the napkins under the plates.

1 With the napkin right side up, fold in half bottom to top. Fold one layer of each upper corner down to the centre line.

2 Unfold the triangle by pulling the point toward you. Rotate the napkin 180 degrees and repeat step 1. Unfold to make a diamond.

3 Fold the four corners in to the centre, making sure the flaps underneath are not allowed to slide out of place.

4 Carefully holding all the flaps in place, turn the napkin over. Fold all the hemmed edges out diagonally from the centre to the corners.

Rose

This beautiful stylized rose, with its cleverly interwoven petals, will sit easily on plates of any size and can be folded successfully using either starched fabric or stiff paper napkins.

1 Arrange the open napkin right side down and fold all four corners to the centre.

2 Turn the napkin over and arrange as a diamond. Fold the lower right-hand sloping edge inward to lie along the horizontal diagonal.

3 Working anticlockwise, repeat step 2 with the next two edges, each overlapping its neighbour.

4 Fold in the final edge, but as you do so turn the flap in on itself and allow to tuck underneath.

5 The design should appear symmetrical. This concept is rather like locking together the four flaps of a cardboard box to keep it closed.

6 Lift up one of the loose corners and pull it across and over the edge of its anti-clockwise neighbour, allowing the pocket formed across the corner to flatten.

7 Once all the flaps have been folded across, this will cause the napkin to form an octagonal shape.

8 Tuck the four loose corners inside the four pockets created by flattening the folds in step 6.

9 Pull out the corners from beneath to suggest extra petals. This move will bring the overall shape back to a square once more.

10 Fold up the small corners at the centre of the rose to create the inner petals.

Pyramid

This spare geometric design makes an elegant treatment for beautiful napkins with an interesting texture or weave, and looks wonderful in a setting of streamlined, modern tableware.

1 Arrange the open napkin right side down and begin by folding all four corners to the centre.

2 Repeat the previous step with the new smaller square.

3 Fold all four corners in to meet at the centre point.

4 Rotate the napkin to form a diamond shape and open out the two right-hand corners.

5 Lift the upper section towards you, and as you do so make an inward fold in the right-hand side to take the top right corner to the bottom right corner.

6 Flatten the inner fold from the apex of the pyramid. You now have a double corner at the lower right-hand side.

7 Fold both layers of the corner as one inside on the existing crease, taking the points to the apex of the pyramid.

8 Turn the napkin over and carefully straighten all the folds before standing it on the table.

Pockets and parcels

Many popular napkin folds create flaps and pockets into which you can tuck anything from a place card to a bread roll. On a buffet table it's convenient to use folded napkins to keep sets of cutlery organized, while ingeniously folded napkins of every size can even conceal a surprise gift for each guest.

Buffet parcel

This practical idea keeps the cutlery tidy and, as it uses two napkins, provides an improvised tablemat as well as a napkin when opened. You will need two napkins of different colours.

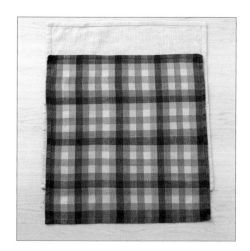

1 Place the two napkins, right sides down, one on top of the other, staggered so that a strip of the lower one is visible at the top.

2 Fold the napkins in half vertically as one, then place the cutlery in the centre and fold the long sides over it.

3 ◁ Pick up the end nearest to you, and fold over about one-third of the roll.

4 ▷ Fold the top end of the roll down and tuck it into the other end.

Picnic set

Use this simple, smart arrangement to keep sets of cutlery and napkins neatly together in a picnic basket or on a party table. You could use a length of ribbon or a raffia tie in place of the napkin ring.

 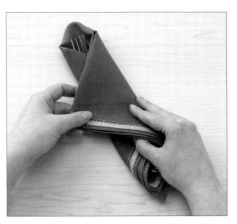 

1 Fold the napkin into quarters. Place the knife and fork in the centre, arranging them diagonally.

2 Wrap the two sides of the napkin around the cutlery.

3 Slide a napkin ring over the bundle to hold the napkin and cutlery in place.

The cable

With its crisp diagonal folds, this rectangular napkin fold looks smart on any dinner table just as it is, but it also has the advantage of creating a pocket into which you can fit a set of cutlery.

1 Fold the napkin into quarters and arrange as a square with the open corners at top right.

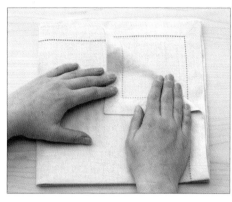

2 Pick up a single layer at the top right corner and fold it at 45 degrees so that the point is at the centre of the square.

3 Double the fold made in the previous step so that the diagonal folded edge lies over the point at the centre.

4 Making the fold on the central diagonal, double this layer over again.

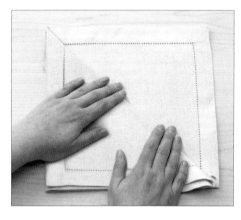

5 Fold the top right corner of the next layer down to the bottom left corner.

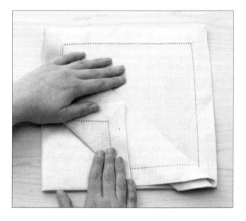

6 Fold this layer back so that the point is touching the centre, as before.

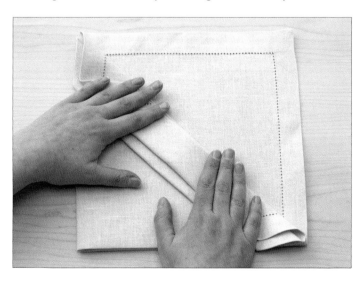

7 Double the fold made in the previous step so that the diagonal folded edge lies over the point at the centre, as in step 3.

8 Double this layer over along the central diagonal. This creates two matching diagonal "stripes" across the napkin.

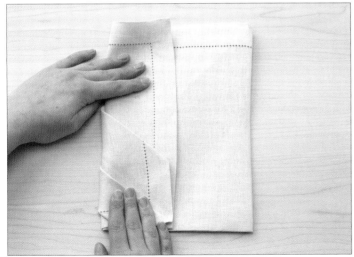

9 Turn the napkin over from side to side. The diagonal folds (now on the underside) run from bottom left to top right. Fold the left-hand vertical edge over to the left by a third.

10 Fold over the right-hand third and tuck the lower corner into the pocket created by the folds in the left-hand section. Turn the napkin over.

Envelope

Use this easy envelope fold to conceal a tiny gift or a few chocolate mints. It looks especially effective if you use napkins with a corner motif, which should be positioned on the right to begin the fold.

1 Arrange the open napkin, right side down, as a diamond. Fold it in half, taking the bottom corner up to the top, and fold in the left-hand side by a third.

2 Fold in the right-hand side so that the sharp point reaches the left-hand corner.

3 Open out the layers of the sharp point now at the bottom left corner and fold it back at the centre to form a small diamond.

4 Fold down the top corner and tuck it into the diamond at the bottom to close the envelope.

Decorative pocket

This clever design makes an attractive pocket in which to place anything from eating implements to a flower. It is another very effective way of displaying napkins with a corner motif.

1 Fold the napkin into quarters, wrong side out, and arrange as a diamond with the open corners at the top. If there is a corner motif, fold the napkin so that it is on the third layer down.

2 Fold down a single layer from the top, leaving a narrow border around the two lower sloping edges.

3 ◁ Fold down the next two layers in the same way, positioning each corner a little above the previous one.

4 ▷ Fold the side corners back, positioning the vertical creases so that they frame the corner motif, and open out the pouch to insert the cutlery.

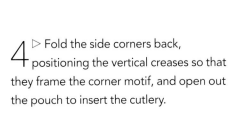

Japanese pleats

The two rolled sections of this fold create a perfect support for a place card and a sprig of leaves or flowers, which soften the strict minimal look. Use a densely woven fabric that will hold the shape.

1 Fold the napkin into thirds to make a rectangular strip. Fold up the left side of the rectangle at 45 degrees so that the vertical folded edge aligns with the centre of the strip.

2 Fold up the right side of the napkin to match the left, then turn the napkin over so that the point is at the top. Roll up the lower flaps tightly until they meet the fold and hold in place with pins.

3 Turn the napkin over again so the point is at the bottom. Fold the left-hand triangle in half, bringing the roll down to the central fold. Repeat with the right-hand side, so that the two rolls lie together and the base is a square. Remove the pins and add a place card and flowers.

Cable buffet

In this compact design the folds of the napkin are securely locked together around the cutlery, allowing guests at a buffet or picnic to help themselves to napkin, knife and fork all at once.

1 Fold the bottom edge of the napkin up to the top, then fold the top of this layer down to the bottom fold.

2 Fold all the layers back up a little way at the bottom and turn the napkin over.

3 Fold the right-hand side of the napkin into the centre. Fold in the left-hand side so that the edges meet.

4 Fold the napkin vertically down the centre, tucking the bottom of one half into the folds on the other. Turn over.

Gift-wrapped

If you are presenting each of your guests with a gift at the table, this is a speedy and flamboyant way to wrap it up. Starch the napkins stiffly so that the corners stand up dramatically.

1 Open the napkin out flat, right side down, and centre the gift on it.

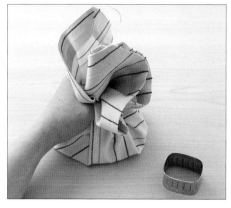

2 Gather the sides of the napkin around the gift, keeping the gathers even and holding all the edges in your hand.

3 Slide a napkin ring over the edges and push it down over the gift to keep the package taut. Adjust the gathers.

Parcelled surprise

This is a neat way to conceal a gift in a square or rectangular box, to give guests a surprise as they open their napkins on celebration days such as Christmas or Easter, or even at a wedding.

1 Arrange the open napkin right side down and position the box diagonally in the centre. Lift two opposite points of the napkin and hold them together.

2 Fold the points over and over again, together, until the fold lies neatly on top of the box.

3 ◁ Fold in the excess fabric at either side of the box and press flat to form a narrow strip.

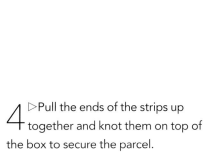

4 ▷ Pull the ends of the strips up together and knot them on top of the box to secure the parcel.

Place card holder

This flat fold makes a compact shape that sits discreetly on the table or on a small plate, and is just the right size to display a place card. It can be made with either fabric or paper napkins.

1 With the open napkin right side down, fold the upper and lower edges into the centre.

2 Fold all four corners at 45 degrees, so that the edges lie along the horizontal centre line.

3 Fold the left-hand side across to the right, making the crease a little further in than the ends of the corner folds.

4 Fold the right-hand side over in the same way, so that there is a symmetrical triangular notch at top and bottom.

5 Turn the napkin over from side to side. Fold the lower edge up by a third, and fold the upper edge down to match.

6 Tuck the two corners of the top flap into the diagonal pockets of the lower portion to hold the folds in place. Finally, tuck the place card inside the diagonal pockets.

Bread basket

Large napkins can be turned into attractive containers. Fold your guests' napkins in this way to hold a bread roll at each place setting, or use a few of these "baskets" to serve crackers or breadsticks.

1 With the napkin arranged as a square, right side down, fold it into thirds, folding the bottom third over the top third.

2 Fold the left-hand edge of the rectangle over toward the right by one-third.

3 Fold the lower side edge of this flap over, again by one-third of the width of the flap. At the folded end of the section the corner rises and does not lie flat.

4 Allow the end of the fold to flatten into a small triangle at the lower left-hand corner of the napkin.

5 Fold the upper third of the left-hand flap down over the previous fold, again flattening the end into a triangle.

6 Fold the narrow strip in the centre out to the left over the triangles.

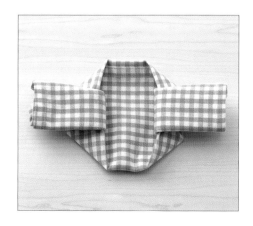

7 Repeat steps 2 to 6 on the right-hand side of the napkin. The design should now appear symmetrical.

8 Place your thumbs inside the basket and open it out while holding the flaps at the ends in place with your fingers.

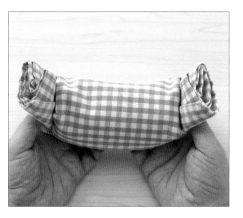

9 Turn the basket over, placing your fingers inside with your thumbs holding the strips in place on the outside.

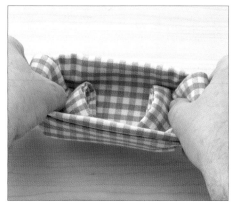

10 Turn the basket inside out, pushing the flaps down inside and bringing the sides up with your fingers.

Index

antiques 7

baskets: bread basket 158–9
bishop's hat 44
bows: bow tie 134–5
  fanned bow 52
bread basket 158–9
breeze 25
buffets: buffet parcel 146
  cable buffet 153
butterfly 94-5

cable 8, 148–9
cable buffet 153
candle fan 92–3
candy cane 14
carousel 9, 124–5
chevrons 8, 66–7
children 79, 98, 99, 100,
    104, 130
china 6
Christmas: Christmas candle
    111
  Christmas star 114–15
  Christmas stocking 112–13
  Christmas tree 110
cicada 74–5
clown's hat 8, 38
cockscomb 8, 32–3
colour: blue and gold 6
concertina pleats 42
coronet 86–7
corsage 90–1
cream horn 68
cutlery 145

decorative pocket 151
diagonal roll 12
diamond 9, 39
diamond breeze 64
dog 99
double fan 50–1
double jabot 8, 62–3
double scroll 15
duck 96–7
duck step 35

Easter bunny 84–5
envelope fold 24
envelope pocket 150

fans 41
  bishop's hat 44
  candle fan 92–3
  diamond breeze 64
  double fan 50–1
  double jabot 8, 62–3
  fan 9, 58–9
  fanned bow 52
  fanned pleats 22
  festival 45
  fire 60–1
  iris in a glass 46
  knotted ribbon 57
  morning sun 49
  palm leaf 48
  parasol 56
  scallop 65
  spiral ribbon 47
  spreading fan 53
  springtime 54–5
festival 45
fire 60–1
fish 108–9
flag 23
flame 9, 101
flowerbud 70–1
folds 11, 117
  bow tie 134–5
  breeze 25
  candy cane 14
  carousel 9, 124–5
  clown's hat 8, 38
  cockscomb 8, 32–3
  diagonal roll 12
  diamond 9, 39
  double scroll 15
  duck step 35
  envelope fold 24
  fanned pleats 22
  flag 23
  folded roll 13
  gathered pleats 18
  geometric style 21
  ice cream cone 20
  knotted napkin 28
  lover's knot 9, 36–7
  mitre 9, 122–3
  nautilus shell 126–7
  nightlight 16
  Oriental fold 138
  overcoat 128–9
  paper heart 19
  papillon 136–7
  pinwheel 130–1
  placemat 139
  pure and simple 31
  pure elegance 34
  pyramid 142–3
  rose 140–1
  sailing boat 30
  scroll 17
  shirt 132–3
  slipper 118–19
  starfish 26
  waterlily 120–1
  wave 9, 27
  wings 29
French lily 8, 76–7

gathered pleats 18
geometric style 21
GI cap 100
gifts 145
  gift-wrapped 154

heart 80
  paper heart 19

ice cream cone 20
iris in a glass 46

Japanese pleats 152

knots 81
  knotted napkin 28
  knotted ribbon 57
  lover's knot 9, 36–7

lover's knot 9, 36–7

mitre 9, 122–3
morning sun 49
Mr Spoon 104-5

napkin rings, pleats 43
nautilus shell 126–7
nightlight 16

ocean liner 106–7
Oriental fold 138
overcoat 128–9

palm leaf 48
paper heart 19
papillon 136–7
parasol 56
parcels 145
  bread basket 158–9
  buffet parcel 146
  gift-wrapped 154
  Japanese pleats 152
  parcelled surprise 155
  picnic set 147
picnic set 147
pinwheel 130–1
place cards 145
  place card holder 156–7
place mat 139
pleats 41
  chevrons 8, 66–7
  cicada 74–5
  concertina pleats 42
  cream horn 68
  fanned pleats 22
  flowerbud 70–1
  French lily 8, 76–7
  gathered pleats 18
  napkin ring 43
  spear 69
  tulip 72–3
pockets 145
  cable 8, 148–9
  cable buffet 153
  decorative pocket 151
  envelope 150
  napkin pocket 151
  place card holder 156–7

pure and simple 31
pure elegance 34
pyramid 142–3

rolled napkins
  diagonal roll 12
  folded roll 13
rose 140–1

sailing boat 30
samurai helmet 102–3
scallop 65
scroll 17
  double scroll 15
shirt 132–3
slipper 118–19
spear 69
special occasions 79
  butterfly 94–5
  candle fan 92–3
  Christmas candle 111
  Christmas star 114–15
  Christmas stocking 112–13
  Christmas tree 110
  coronet 86–7
  corsage 90–1
  dog 99
  duck 96–7
  Easter bunny 84–5
  fish 108–9
  flame 9, 101
  GI cap 100
  heart 80
  knot 81
  Mr Spoon 104–5
  ocean liner 106–7
  samurai helmet 102–3
  swan 88–9
  turbo 98
  Valentine rose 82–3
spiral ribbon 47
spreading fan 53
springtime 54–5
starfish 26
swan 88–9

table settings 79
tulip 72–3
turbo 98

Valentine rose 82–3

waterlily 120–1
wave 9, 27
wings 29
wrapping food 145